Understanding Sports Culture

Tony Schirato

SAGE Publications

Los Angeles • London • New Delhi • Singapore

First published 2007

SAGE Publications Ltd
1 Oliver's Yard
55 City Road
London EC1Y 1SP

SAGE Publications Inc.
2455 Teller Road
Thousand Oaks, California 91320

SAGE Publications India Pvt Ltd
B 1/I 1 Mohan Cooperative Industrial Area
Mathura Road
New Delhi 110 044

SAGE Publications Asia-Pacific Pte Ltd
33 Pekin Street #02-01
Far East Square
Singapore 048763

British Library Cataloguing in Publication data

A catalogue record for this book is available from the
British Library

ISBN 978-1-4129-0738-5
ISBN 978-1-4129-0739-2 (pbk)

Library of Congress Control Number: 2006933757

Typeset by Keyword Group Ltd
Printed in Great Britain by Athenaeum Press
Printed on paper from sustainable resources

Dedicated to the memory of Pierre Bourdieu

Acknowledgements

I would like to acknowledge the contributions of the following people: Joost de Bruin, Anita Brady, Jim Collinge, Sean Cubitt, Trisha Dunleavy, Annemarie Jutel, Thierry Jutel, Harry Ricketts, Geoff Stahl and Jen Webb. A special thanks to Mary Roberts for her very detailed feedback and support.

Contents

1 Introduction: Playing Sport

There's a Nike television commercial that neatly encapsulates the relation between the notion of play and the contemporary cultural field of sport. The setting is a soccer match between the national teams of Brazil and Portugal. As the players walk, side-by-side, through the concrete subterranean passage that leads onto the field, the scene is clearly recognizable as early twenty-first-century sport, characterized by strong capitalist, bureaucratic and media inflections. The sides (selected by managers appointed by the respective national federations) are wearing national colours, with the shirts supplied by multinational sports companies (Brazil, for instance, have signed a long-term contract, and are closely associated, with Nike). Many of the players – Roberto Carlos, the Ronaldos, Figo, Ronaldinho – are instantly recognizable worldwide as players and media stars. They are frequently the subject of news stories about transfer rumours or romances, and appear in advertisements for football boots or upcoming games. Nike's choice of teams reflects those media and business logics: Brazil and Portugal have numerous high profile footballers, and share a tradition of playing and valuing skilful, non-ends-directed football – in contrast to national teams such as Germany, England and even Italy and Argentina, which have usually adopted a more cynical approach. One of the criticisms made of the highly talented Portugese team, for instance, is that they are more interested in playing with the ball than scoring goals; and similarly it was often said of Brazil (until repeated failures at the World Cup in the seventies and eighties caused something of a change of heart and tactics) that they would rather 'play beautifully and lose' than resort to 'ugly' football (playing defensively, systematically fouling the opposition).

The occasion is clearly an important competition match sanctioned by FIFA. The players' faces and bodies show signs of seriousness and tension: they process slowly and deliberately, stare intently ahead, and are too focused to acknowledge the other team. They emerge from the tunnel and take the field in a modern stadium (perhaps with a retractable roof) filled with as many as one hundred thousand (the capacity of the stadium having been determined, among other things, by safety regulations and requirements) seated fans who will have paid the equivalent of something in the region of hundreds (legally) and thousands (to scalpers) of US dollars a seat, depending on the importance of the match and the location of the seats. Some of the more desirable seating will be located in corporate boxes owned or rented by large corporations for the entertainment of their business clients, who will be provided with restaurant-quality meals and drinks. The game will be strictly circumscribed regarding temporal, spatial and material characteristics and dimensions. Action will begin, cease and recommence only when the referee blows a whistle, and will take place within a marked space commensurate with FIFA rules regarding the length and breadth of the field and its various components (the dimensions of the penalty area, the height of the goalposts). The game will usually run for ninety minutes (not including time added on for stoppages), even if the result is a foregone conclusion after thirty minutes and supporters of the losing team are leaving in droves. Players must wear appropriate gear: to wear the wrong-coloured shorts, or only one sock, or with writing or other marks on the gear other than those of the official or recognized sponsors or makers, would result in a player being removed (temporarily or otherwise) from the field. And this applies to bodies as well, in the case of, say, an injury that causes bleeding, or of the exposure of a player's buttocks to the crowd to communicate a (presumably very brief) political message.

There will be a strict demarcation between officials and players, and players and spectators. The media may purport to 'take viewers into the middle of the action', but if a spectator somehow climbed over the partition that separated them from the players and evaded the numerous trained security staff and police and ran onto the field, then they'd be chased, apprehended, ejected from the ground and heavily fined. The crowd at the venue will be joined by hundreds of millions of viewers around the world watching and listening to it on live and delayed telecasts, through both terrestrial and satellite media, on television, radio and through the internet. A pre-game show will analyze past results, injuries and the possible influence of the referee on the outcome. Highlights of previous games will be accompanied by a plethora of statistics (team and individual) about passes-per-shot-at-goal, goals-per-game, time-in-possession, tackles, fouls, goals and assists (although this will be paltry in comparison to the statistical information provided by networks covering, say, a World Series baseball game). Every significant action (offside decisions, fouls, goals) will be replayed, in slow motion and at ordinary speed and from numerous angles, both on a large screen within the stadium (broken only by sponsorship messages), and to media viewers; and remote microphones will pick up the noises and words coming from the players and officials. At halftime a panel of experts (made up of past and current players and managers, as well as journalists and media commentators) will analyze incidents, provide opinions about what is happening and why, and predict the outcome. The match receipts will be in the tens of millions of US dollars, but this will be dwarfed by the television and internet rights, and the advertising revenue generated by board space around the ground, or the right to exclusively kit one or both teams. The players will be paid out of this revenue, as will the federations, managers, coaches, physios, doctors, publicists, agents, halftime entertainers, the singer of the respective national anthems, and the referee and linespersons. Once the game has finished, it will continue to be analyzed and to generate income: television networks around the world will show highlights during the sports segment of the evening news; newspapers and magazines will write stories about the game and its dramas, heroes and villains; videos and DVDs of the game will be produced, packaged, advertised and sold. Reputations will be made and lost (with important consequences for salaries, contract extensions and sponsorship revenue), players will be induced to change clubs, and millions of fans will celebrate or drink away or violently manifest their sorrow, depending on the outcome. Politicians will line up to be photographed with the winners, and questions asked in the media and political institutions of the losing country. A government might even fall as a consequence of the result.

Little of this is actually shown in the commercial: most of it is implied through what we see in those opening shots. Sporting advertisements usually mirror or reproduce, in miniature, the field and its practices, values, rules, agents and institutions, with the stars, drama, excitement, crowd and skill of the game condensed into a few visuals. A typical football commercial would show a star like Ronaldo or Beckham on the ball, a scything tackle being skilfully avoided, the winning goal blasted into the back of the net past an acrobatic goalkeeper, the celebrations of the players, the fans shouting and screaming with joy. And the name of the sponsor would be associated with the action, the players and the gear, but also with the passion, excitement and beauty of football.

But this isn't a typical sporting commercial. Let's go back to the scene we were describing: Brazil and Portugal are on their way to take part in an institutionally authorized, important and very serious sporting contest, when the players start behaving as if they were children or teenagers having a kickabout on a Brazilian beach. One player takes possession of the ball and starts playing with it – juggling it, bouncing it off walls, flicking it up into the air. The rest join in, trying to get the ball away from the first player in order to outdo his tricks. The intensity, pace and skill increases as each person ups the ante, until the action resembles a pinball game, with the ball flying in all directions. Suddenly the referee appears. He's clearly horrified by what's going on, tackles (actually fouls) the player in possession (the Brazilian Ronaldo) and retrieves the ball. The final scene shows that the order of things has been restored: the dignified-looking referee holds the ball, a national anthem plays, the crowd sings, the cameras pan across the players who are now literally back in line, hands behind their backs. They are blackened, dirty, dishevelled and chastened, but focused and in possession of themselves: playtime is over, and sport takes its place.

To some extent this book reprises this narrative: it's primarily about the development of what we understand as the modern field of sport, and its transformation into a form of popular culture closely tied in with, and in many ways indistinguishable from, the values, logics and discourses associated with bureaucracy, global capitalism, the media and more generally the field of power (Bourdieu 1998). But it's also about the relationship between sport and the disposition to play, and what we might call the meta-narrative of the Nike commercial – which is that even when the field of sport is at its most business-like, trying to exclude the spontaneity and wastefulness associated with playful activity (represented by the figure of the referee restoring the seriousness of sport), simultaneously it has to cover itself by producing performances of its commitment to the idea that, at heart, sport is still just people at play.

2 Theories of Play, Games and Sport

INTRODUCTION

A child building a sandcastle on the beach, someone doodling on a notepad in a long meeting, and a worker using company time to play fantasy sports: these are all activities that are commensurate with George Bataille's notion of a 'general economy', which he defines as "a play of energy which has no end limits" (1989: 23). Bataille differentiates general economy from specific economic systems, which are understood as "particular operations with limited ends" (22). The aforementioned activities appear to have no systematic or rational utility, or at the very least the potential gains associated with them (for instance, as a form of training) seem insignificant. The necessary articulation that is presumed, within a closed economy, between expenditure and growth (understood here as deriving an advantage or benefit – for instance learning a useful skill, or acquiring some form of cultural or financial capital) has only a tenuous relationship with the activities of building a sandcastle, doodling or the impromptu performance of a dance. General economy, on the other hand, offers an entirely different narrative with regard to this question of expenditure, one that is predicated not on gain but on loss:

> As soon as we act reasonably we want to consider the utility of our actions; utility implies ... maintenance of growth. Now if it is necessary to respond to exuberance, it is no doubt possible to use it for growth. But ... supposing there is no longer any growth possible, what is to be done with the seething energy that remains? To waste it is obviously not to use it. And yet, what we have is a draining-away, a pure and simple loss, which occurs in any case: from the first, the excess energy, if it cannot be used for growth, is lost. (30–1)

In other words, waste and loss are not entirely removed from any connection with utility. The pleasure and/or desire that characterizes processes of waste and loss, and which is implied in Bataille's statement that "life starts only with the deficit of ... systems ... order and reserve has meaning only from the moment the ordered and reserved forces liberate and lose themselves for ends that cannot be subordinated to anything one can account for" (1989: 128), is clearly commensurate with and helps us explicate the apparent paradox that is play, which builds routines and structures in order to escape from them.

An aspect of Bataille's work that is particularly relevant to our understanding of the disposition to play is bound up with his interest (following Marcel Mauss, Johan Huizinga and Roger Caillois) in the phenomenon of potlatch. Bataille's reading of potlatch, which is perhaps best described as a systematic and apparently pointless destruction or gifting of wealth, is that it is a loss (goods are destroyed) disguised as a form of utility (the loss acquires capital) that is in fact a disguised loss (nothing is produced). But the real theoretical or exemplary value of potlatch, for Bataille and other theorists of play, is that it is an obvious instance of the community being played (by a very powerful disposition), rather than the other way round. In other words, although the community may produce all kinds of explanations of and rationales about potlatch and similar processes which appear to place agency back in their hands ('it really does have a utility'; 'we're only doing this to garner prestige and capital'), in fact it is the community which is being played (along). Play, from this perspective, is a disposition that inhabits or passes through sites, in different forms and intensities at different times, but which is often explained in terms of individual or even communal agency.

THEORIZING PLAY

The notion that play inhabits and animates individuals and communities, and continues to exert a strong socio-cultural presence even in its apparent absence, is one of a number of important insights derived from the work of Johan Huizinga. Huizinga explains the notion of play as both a universal abstraction (he posits that it is not only prior to culture – it effectively animates it) and a historically situated disposition-as-practice. Play, for Huizinga:

> is older than culture (and) ... more than a mere physiological phenomenon or a
> psychological reflex ... It is a significant function ... that is to say, there is some

sense to it. In play there is something 'at play' which transcends the immediate needs of life and imparts meaning to the action. All play means something. If we call the active principle that makes up the essence of play 'instinct', we explain nothing. (1966: 1)

This quote identifies two fundamental characteristics of play. First, it "is a thing of its own" (3): it is has no biological purpose, doesn't "serve something which is not play" (2), and is possessed of its own generic qualities. It gives rise to an infinite number of socio-cultural manifestations and transformations, but always within a strictly limited regime of characteristics, imperatives and qualities. Second, although play has no moral or ethical function, it is both a catalyst for imaginative activity and stands in opposition to a mood or culture of seriousness. That play is opposed to seriousness does not mean, however, that it can't be an intense activity: the disposition to play has the capacity to possess people and move them out of or away from their everyday duties and responsibilities. In order to deal with this and other apparent contradictions (on the one hand play is opposed to seriousness/play can be serious; on the other play is free/we are played) that arise from Huizinga's account of play, we need to consider his contextual analysis, located at the end of *Homo Ludens*, of what he calls the "play element in contemporary civilization" (195).

As well as being self-serving and opposed to seriousness, play has, for Huizinga, six generic aspects: it is voluntary or freely adopted; disinterested and irreducible to any utility; distinct or sequestered from ordinary life; creates and demands adherence to order (through the adoption of rules or patterns of behaviour); operates under temporal and spatial limits; and is either representational or competitive in some respect. Huizinga provides elaborate descriptions, definitions and examples of what he means by these terms, but the key to reading, explicating and grounding play-as-practice is his argument that, from the nineteenth century on, play atrophies (198). In other words, it is easier to recognize more precisely what Huizinga means by play, and to reconcile its apparent contradictions, once we know what kinds of socio-historical forces and tendencies 'send it away'.

When Huizinga uses the term 'contemporary civilization', he is in effect referring to nineteenth-century industrial Britain and its legacies. One of the most significant of those legacies is modern sport, and it is here that the differentiation between play and its other is, for Huizinga, most pronounced:

Now, with the increasing systematization and regimentation of sport, something of the pure play-quality is inevitably lost ... In modern social life sport occupies a place alongside and apart from the cultural process ... The ability of modern social techniques to stage mass demonstrations with the maximum of outward show in the field of athletics does not alter the fact that neither the Olympiads nor the organized sports of American Universities nor the loudly trumpeted international contests have, in the smallest degree, raised sport to the level of a culture-creating activity. However important it may be for players or spectators, it remains sterile. The old play-factor has undergone almost complete atrophy. (197–8)

There are three factors in Huizinga's account of modern sport that differentiate it from play, and the first and by far the most important of these is that it is derived from a world-view that is essentially utilitarian and rationalist. In Huizinga's account play is of and for itself, rather than a means to an end; and while play may take itself seriously, it doesn't extend that privilege – a rejection that is reciprocated by a utilitarian mindset. Everything follows from this, and cleaves a path between play and sport. Football players may take the field voluntarily, but if the dominant motivation behind their play is financial gain or to improve their fitness, then they aren't playing. Similarly, although there is order in, and spatial and temporal limitations to, a kick-about amongst players in a park (they may tacitly agree to take turns in kicking, one may act as goalkeeper while the others take shots, shots at goal should be from about the edge of the penalty area) that is a very different situation from the necessary adherence, on the part of professional footballers, to the exact iterations and regularities articulated in a FIFA rulebook.

For Huizinga, two additional factors – capitalism, and what we can refer to, after Foucault (1997), as the reason of state – contribute to this differentiation of play from sport. Although both are clearly derived from a utilitarian/rationalist world-view, they take different socio-cultural forms. The economies of time and effort that go into the creation and maintenance of the play-civilization nexus (Huizinga writes that "civilization is, in its earliest phases, played ... it arises in and as play, and never leaves it" (173) are untenable within a capitalist order: if time is money, there is no place for the unproductive use of time. With the reason of state we are in different territory. When Huizinga writes about "the ability of modern social techniques to stage mass demonstrations with the maximum of outward show in the field of athletics" (198) he is clearly referring to state-managed spectacles such as the 1936 Berlin Olympics: here the investment of time and effort is an investment in the maintenance and/or accumulation of prestige, or the training, disciplining and pacification of the state's bodies and minds.

Although *Homo Ludens* purports to provide a socio-historical explanation of play, it is difficult not to read that narrative as more mythical than historical, with the prototype being that of a fall from some kind of golden age. The problem with this account, in which play more or less succumbs to, and is atrophied by, historical forces and developments, is that it contradicts Huizinga's thesis that "civilization is ... played ... it arises in and as play, and never leaves it" (173). What is implied here is that play is a disposition that inhabits not just people and places but, as Huizinga admits, world-views and institutions that are entirely antithetical to it. He devotes a small section of *Homo Ludens* to a discussion of business as play, but never seriously pursues the line of enquiry, which logically follows from his own premises, that capitalism (and for that matter the workings of the reason of state) arises from, and is characterized by, a strong sense of play.

This aporia in Huizinga's account of play is picked up and addressed by Roger Caillois in his book *Men, Play and Games* (2001). Caillois demonstrates how play, which he defines, following Huizinga, as being in opposition to and of a different order from institutionalized socio-cultural activities, comes to be 'two things at once' – simultaneously work and its antithesis:

> Play ... creates no wealth or goods, thus differing from work ... play is an occasion of pure waste: waste of time, energy, ingenuity, skill, and often of money ... Play must be defined as a free and voluntary activity, a source of joy and amusement. A game which one would be forced to play ... would become constraint ... from which one would strive to be free. As an obligation or simply an order, it would lose one of its basic characteristics: the fact that the player devotes himself spontaneously to the game, of his free will and for his own pleasure, each time completely free to choose retreat, silence, meditation, idle solitude, or creative activity ... (play occurs) only when the players have a desire to play ... in order to find diversion, escape from responsibility and routine ... In effect play is essentially a separate occupation, carefully isolated from the rest of life (5–6).

Caillois accepts that authentic play is separated-off from much of ordinary life because of its non-productive (art does not count as play because it produces material goods) and volitional (professional sportspersons are working, not playing) nature. But he recognizes that those material and historical contexts of ordinary life (the workplace, post-industrial society) are both what is being escaped from, and the sites of escape.

PLAY, GAMES AND SPORT

In *From Ritual to Record* (1978) Allen Guttmann traces a line from play to games to what we understand as (modern) sport. Guttmann insists that these groups of activities cannot be differentiated in material or technical terms; for instance "the tombs of Beni Hassan in Egypt, dating from

Pharaonic times, depict very nearly the entire gamut of wrestling holds used in today's intercollegiate matches" (11). He continues:

> In other words, it is doubtful that the kind of game, determined by anthropologists, matters as much as the cultural perception of the game on the part of the players themselves. We can learn a great deal from careful attention to the games a society emphasizes, but the 'same' game is likely to vary greatly in meaning from one cultural context to another. (11)

Making use of the concept of play, games or sport to categorize an activity is one obvious way of inflecting or determining its meaning; but such practices are complicated because the concept of sport stands in relation to the other two terms in a rather ambiguous way. There is what we might call a cognate relation between them: sport is derived from play and games, and sporting institutions continue to represent this relationship as fundamental to the authenticity and attraction of professional sport. At the same time the field of sport and its activities occupy a much more significant and elevated place within the contemporary socio-cultural world than play and games, which are often treated as trivial or insignificant in comparison.

Guttmann treats games as a particular version of play:

> Play can be divided into two categories – spontaneous play and organized play, which we call games ... spontaneous play may be as close as we can ever come to the realm of pure freedom, but most play is regulated and rule-bound. It remains nonutilitarian ... but games symbolize the willing surrender of absolute spontaneity for the sake of playful order. (1978: 4)

He goes on to subdivide games into two further categories – activities and contests. There are a variety of games which are non-competitive and emphasize involvement, aesthetics, technical competency, skill or the completion of a set of tasks (Guttmann refers to leap frog, ring-around-the-rosie, playing doctor and the ceremonial Japanese game of kemari), while contests are clearly more closely related to sport, because of their "apparent stress on winning" (5). Sport differs from games because it "includes an important measure of physical as well as intellectual skill" (7). It is a particular form and extension of both play and games, joined to them by a lack of utility that also differentiates sporting contests from the kind of agonistics found in the courtroom or on the battlefield. There is nothing in this definition, however, to differentiate sport from theatre or dancing, or any number of activities not conventionally associated with the field of sport. Guttmann suggests that:

> The distinction ... may lie in the theory of expression ... the arts can be conceived of as modes of expression which, in their untruncated form, assume the

communication of artist with an audience ... art must communicate something – a sense of form or color, an awareness of patterned sound, an interpretation of human movement. The artist needs his audience ... Games, contests, and even sports do acquire audiences and no one familiar with modern professional sports is unaware of the intimate financial relationship between sports, live audiences, and the television networks. Nonetheless, sports have existed, do exist, and will continue to exist in situations without an audience. (11–12)

This account has two significant deficiencies. First, there are clearly some activities which fit this criteria ("playful nonutilitarian contests which includes an important measure of physical as well as intellectual skill") that have no status as sport: Guttmann refers to dancing, but there are also less obvious but equally anomalous examples like stilt fighting, dwarf throwing, jelly wrestling, tree climbing, wife carrying, log rolling, eating contests, egg and spoon races and various forms of 'playing chicken'. Second, the differentiation of sport from the arts and other cultural forms, based on the principle of sport lacking an imperative to communicate with or perform for an audience (Guttmann goes even further than identifying this as an absence: he suggests that 'display' or performing for the fans "violates the code of sports" (12), was probably untenable in the nineteenth century; but it would be impossible to apply this characterization to modern, media and business dominated sport-as-spectacle where players, sports journalists, administrators and businesspeople are ever mindful of the need to attract and entertain audiences. In short, Guttmann's definitions and argument don't account for the ways in which cultural fields simultaneously cross over into one another without losing their field-specific inflections or character. As Norbert Elias writes in *Quest for Excitement*:

> The setting of sport, like that of many other leisure pursuits, is designed to move, to stir the emotions, to evoke tensions in the form of a controlled, a well-tempered excitement without the risks and tensions usually connected with excitement in other life-situations, a 'mimetic' excitement which can be enjoyed and which may have a liberating, cathartic effect, even though the emotional resonance to the imaginary design contains, as it usually does, elements of anxiety, fear – or despair. But while sport shares with many other leisure pursuits its mimetic character, an ability to stir emotions akin to those experienced in other situations ... it differs from most others and especially from the arts by the central part played in all sports by struggles *in toto* between living human beings. In all kinds of sport, living human beings struggle with each other directly or indirectly. (1993b: 48–9)

Why is it that activities or games that appear to fulfil Guttmann's (and indeed Elias and Dunning's) criteria are not generally treated, understood or categorized as sport? The answer is that what constitutes sport is largely dealt within and determined by the relation between the field of sport and the wider socio-cultural field (with particular regard needing to be paid to institutions and agents from powerful fields such as government, business and the media). Events, meanings, shifts of power and changes to ideas, values, logics and institutions arise out of the imbrication of these two regimes: what Bourdieu refers to as the field of power (1998) influences and inflects individual fields (although this varies depending on the extent to which each field is autonomous or heteronomous, to again use Bourdieu's terms), but the interactions between people and institutions within each field are also field-specific. So the form taken by cricket in the nineteenth century was tied in with the wider socio-political development of what Elias refers to as "the free association of gentlemen" (1993a: 39) who "formed clubs (and) agreed on the unification of local traditions" (39). One of these clubs, the MCC, went on to control, co-ordinate and shape other local and international organizations and competitions in terms of its own image and values.

SPORT AND THE CIVILIZING PROCESS

Perhaps the most influential account of the genesis of the field of sport within and in relation to wider socio-cultural and historical contexts is to be found in Elias' *The Civilizing Process* (2000). Elias analyzes and contextualizes sport by way of a concept he calls figurational sociology, which understands social activity and change as a series of necessarily interdependent processes. For Elias, historical change:

> is not 'rationally' planned; but neither is it a random coming and going of orderless patterns. How does it happen at all that formations arise in the human world that no single human being has intended ... plans and actions, the emotional and rational impulses of individual people, constantly interweave in a friendly or hostile way. This basic tissue resulting from many single plans and actions of people can give rise to changes and patterns that no individual person has planned or created. From this interdependence of people arises an order sui generis, an order more compelling and stronger than the will and the reason of the individual people composing it. It is this order of interweaving human impulses and strivings, this social order, which determines the course of historical change. (365–6)

From this theoretical perspective, people, concepts and events are (only) explicable as pluralities, as mutually dependent (and temporally and spatially specific) structures; in other words sport can't be conceived as a transcendental or ahistorical phenomenon, or as an activity that precedes the wider socio-cultural field. Instead Elias suggests that sport first appears in its modern form in England in the late eighteenth century, although the impetus for its development can be traced back even further, to Western Europe in the late Middle Ages, which coincide with the advent of what he refers to as the civilizing process. The civilizing process "does not follow a straight line" and is subject to "diverse criss-cross movements, shifts and spurts" (157), but:

> if we consider the movement over large time spans, we see clearly how the com-
> pulsions arising directly from the threat of weapons and physical force have
> gradually diminished, and how those forms of dependency which lead to the
> regulation of the affects in the form of self-control, gradually increased ...
> restraint ... is enforced less and less by direct physical force. It is cultivated in
> individuals from an early age as habitual self-restraint by the structure of social
> life, by the pressure of social institutions in general, and by certain executive
> organs of society ... in particular. (157–8)

Elias contends that evidence of a connection between the incipient civilizing processes of the late Middle Ages and the development of modern sport can be seen in the gradual transformation of the class-specific physical games and contests (that often resulted in large-scale fatalities) that served to train knights in the techniques of fighting into the stylized, orchestrated, regulated and often international tournaments and jousts of the Renaissance. At the same time this influence hardly extended outside the court: popular sports (such as the variants of folk football) continued to be local, unregulated, undifferentiated, spontaneous, disorganized, brutal and violent.

According to Elias the main catalyst for the development of modern sport was the socio-political change that took place in England in the seventeenth century, following the Civil War and the defeat of the monarchy. The subsequent mediation of political conflict and violence by parliamentary and state controlled bureaucratic institutions and procedures (and the appropriation, on the part of the state, of a monopoly with regard to the use of legitimate forms of violence) gave rise to standardized and regulated rules of behaviour and conduct, and institutions and apparatuses which oversaw their implementation and compliance, as well as the voluntary associations and organizations that represented particular social, cultural and political orientations or identities. Once this phenomenon was extended to physical games and activities we have the beginnings of what Elias calls sportization, which is understood as the development, within sport, of codes of conduct and values commensurate with the imperatives of the civilizing process. From the late eighteenth century onward:

> the framework of rules applying to sport became stricter, including those rules
> attempting to provide for fairness and equal chance for all to win. The rules

governing sport became more precise, more explicit, written down and more differentiated and supervision of rule-observance became more efficient. Moreover, in the course of the same process, self-control and self-discipline increased, while in the game-contests which became known as sports a balance was established between the possibility of attaining a high level of combat-tension and what was then seen as a reasonable protection against injury. (Murphy *et al.* 2002: 95)

The advent of widespread consumerism and regimes of fashion, increased disposable income, and specific changes to class-relations coincided with activities such as horseracing, boxing and cricket attracting large crowds drawn from all sectors of society; widespread gambling on sporting contests; and sport starting to take on institutionally authorized iterative forms (regarding rules, equipment, designations, calendars and events) that are recognizably modern. Similarly the more dramatic socio-historical changes of the nineteenth century (including industrialization, mass urbanization, widespread public education and improvements in communication and transport) occurred at the same time as the development of professional football and the modern sporting ethos that is associated with cricket, rugby and athletics.

To what extent can we presume a necessary articulation between the material and technological changes that characterized these periods and the rise of and changes to sporting practices, institutions and values? In other words, was the advent of professional football in England in the nineteenth century, for instance, little more than a by-product of the configuration of specific communication and transport technologies (newspapers, the railways) and wider socio-economic developments (the spread of capitalism and industrialization, mass education). There are two main problems with this proposition. First, it is predicated on a kind of determinism that effectively abstracts technology from the socio-historical conditions and processes that are constitutive of it. Second, technological or economic change can't explain why association football became the pre-eminent spectator sport in Britain in the nineteenth century and in Europe and South America in the twentieth century, while failing to achieve a similar status in the United States, Canada, Australia or New Zealand. Football emerges from the process of sportization to become a leisure pursuit and a mode of training upper-class English schoolboys in leadership and ethics, and then changes into an international and professional game increasingly oriented towards issues of spectatorship, media coverage and commercial viability. None of this was necessary or pre-ordained. Football and sport in general are first and foremost a set of possibilities, and developments in any cultural field, including that of sport, are always simultaneously the result of an ongoing relationship between wider socio-historical forces and a set of logics and agonistics specific to that field. This insight allows us, in Bourdieu's words:

> to grasp the specificity of sporting practice, or, more precisely, to determine how certain pre-existing physical exercises, or others which may have received a radically new meaning and function ... became sports, defined with respect to their rewards, their rules, and also the social identity of their participants – players or spectators – by the specific logic of the 'sporting field'. (1993a: 119)

Elias' formulation of the relation between the civilizing process and sport provides us with a useful explanation for making sense of the development and functions of modern sport, but it is necessary to put up several qualifications, mostly of the kind identified by Murphy *et al.* (2002). They reject the criticism that the theory of a civilizing process is based on a "latent evolutionism" (101), mainly by citing Elias' numerous references to decivilizing phases, counter movements and the non-linear nature of social change. What they fail to address, however, is the evolutionary function and status ascribed within the civilizing process to self-control, a term that is, for Elias, more or less synonymous with civilization. The equating of self-control with the civilizing process means that the former takes on the (de facto) role of an abstraction or ideal that doesn't quite drive or animate socio-historical events (progress is not inevitable), but civilization is unthinkable without it. At the same time this ideal is given a very strong class inflection: the civilized habitus is almost always acquired by dominant or upper-class groups, who are more likely to be 'equipped' with "sufficient self-control for containing excitement" (1993b: 54). This class-specific dimension of the notion of self-control is largely elided by Elias (he characterizes it "as a symptom of some defect in society at large rather than simply in that one particular sector" (1993b: 54), but its presence makes the civilizing process narrative read like a historical version of the trickle-down theory of economics. In effect, Elias is caught up in the process of making universal claims for activities that seem to serve specific interests. The political changes that occurred in England in the eighteenth century (particularly parliamentarization) had winners (the land-owning classes, who gained control of English politics) and losers (Elias refers (1993b: 30) to the disappearance and annihilation of the free English peasantry after the enclosure movement had succeeded); but the symbolic and physical violence that characterized this social agonistics are in a sense 'irrelevant' precisely because they result from and give added impetus to the civilized and civilizing game of parliamentarization. Elias never focuses on the power that accrues to gentlemen as a result of the naturalizing and valorizing of gentlemanly behaviour (largely via the public school system), or "ask who benefits and who suffers from the monopoly of the state over legitimate violence, and ... of the dominance wielded through the state" (Bourdieu 1992: 93). This explains, to some extent, why Elias' work on the development of sport in nineteenth-century England, and the relation between parliamentarization and sportization, lacks a political focus or dimension. Elias is not particularly interested in how the development of cricket as an institutionalized sport functioned as an adjunct to the maintenance of the symbolic violence that constituted the English class system. Rather he is concerned to identify and plot the structural relations between the social and its specific fields, and to be able to show "whether and when the development of (cricket) reached the level of several local clubs, of a national association coordinating all clubs, and ... the development of several national associations with an international association coordinating them". (Elias 1993b: 39)

SPORT AS IDEOLOGY AND COMMODITY

The relatively apolitical nature of Elias' work is antithetical to Marxist accounts of sport, society and history, which understand the historical processes that produce the civilized state as a continuation, by other means, of class warfare; and which treats sport (at least within capitalist cultures) as a form of work and/or an important ideological site or apparatus for inculcating capitalist values. In *Sport – A Prison of Measured Time* Jean-Marie Brohm (1978) argues that the core values and principles of capitalism – agonistics and struggle, virility, physical and symbolic violence, physical dominance, chauvinism, racism and sexism – are learned and embodied through sport, either as a bodily hexis that is acquired from playing or as a set of dispositions that are naturalized through spectatorship and identification (15). And Bero Rigauer posits a relatively straightforward and analogous relationship between sport and modern forms of labour:

> In modern industrial society, certain techniques of productive work have become such dominant models of conduct that they impose their norms even upon so-called leisure-time activities. Sport has not been able to escape this imposition of norms. (1981: 1)

At an amateur level, sport trains bodies to become consumers and capitalists; at a professional level, it both reproduces capitalist alienation of the labourer *qua* labour and operates as a "new opiate of the people" (Brohm 1978: 7). By and large the dominant (and usually strongly institutionalized) culture in schools and youth sport is one of playing purely for results, which effectively devalues non-competitive behaviour; and this culture is even more pervasive (to the point of foreclosing any other possibilities or ways of thinking) in professional sport. So children who grow up watching, idolizing and imitating sports stars learn and naturalize the notion that life is, and is meant to be, a Darwinian exercise. At the same time it would be untenable to characterize children's sport as pure inculcation. When children and adolescents participate in organized sports (football, netball, athletics, cricket, baseball) or in make-up games (touch rugby, a kick-about using makeshift goals) they are being subjected, at some level, to a form of socio-cultural training (learning to win, to compete, to struggle and overcome). But they are also playing in order to escape from the routines of schoolwork; various forms of symbolic violence (racism, ethnic- and class-based prejudice); and the regimentation of family life.

There are different histories and traditions of the involvement of capitalist logics and values in sport. American sports leagues in the nineteenth century, for instance, were usually founded by entrepreneurs, while British leagues had more varied points of departure, often brought into existence by core groups which included representatives from clubs, community groups, schools and universities. In Britain, Australia and New Zealand in the nineteenth century – and indeed up until the second half of the twentieth century and later – sport was never entirely professional even at the highest levels. Some players in certain sports or leagues (for instance, W.G. Grace in cricket) earned substantial amounts of money, but this was usually a supplement to some other form of income. Moreover, the tendency to commoditize players and in a sense abstract their relation to the team or club as a (temporary) work arrangement – so common today, with frequent transfers between football teams, or the wholesale purchasing of a team by the Abramovich-backed Chelsea – was a relatively rare occurrence prior to the 1960s, at least outside the United States of America. In fact the obvious intervention of business or financial interests in sport was often forbidden or regarded as a form of negative cultural capital: professionals had a lower social status than amateurs in cricket, and soccer players transferring to another team were often regarded as mercenaries.

Historical evidence makes it difficult to sustain Brohm's reading that sport is only explicable within the context of a necessary articulation from the ownership of the means of production (that is, at the level of base) down to the wider socio-cultural field (the superstructure). An alternative theoretical approach that maintains the Marxist emphasis on the relation between cultural activity and political economy, while moving beyond the limitations of the base/superstructure model, can be found in the work of the Russian Marxist V.N. Volosinov. Volosinov rejected the presumption that Russian novels such as *War and Peace* and *Crime and Punishment* were simply ideological symptoms. The specific example he uses is Turgenev's mid-nineteenth century novel *Rudin*, which introduced the concept of the 'superfluous man' into Russian culture. Volosinov's point was that even if there was a strong connection between economics and literary representations, this hardly explained choices made at the level of content, genre or narrative styles. He writes that:

> Even if a correspondence established is correct, even if it is true that 'superfluous men' did appear in literature in connection with the breakdown of the economic structure of the gentry, still, for one thing it does not at all follow that related economic upsets mechanically cause 'superfluous men' to be produced on the pages of a novel ... for another thing, the correspondence established itself remains without any cognitive value until both the specific role of the 'superfluous man' in the artistic structure of the novel and the specific role of the novel in social life are elucidated. (1986: 18)

In other words, while socio-historical conditions and contexts allow for the possibility of the representation of a particular type of character, what finally determines the literary form of this representation is a combination of the logics, imperatives and politics of the literary field and the different kinds of articulations between that field and society.

To demonstrate how these relations and logics are played out, we can draw a structural analogy between the emergence of the superfluous man in Russian literature and that of the English football star David Beckham in the field of professional sport. It would be easy to explain the rise of Beckham as a symptom of the malaise of sport (the colonization of a working-class sport by advertising and the media, leading to its incorporation into commodity culture) which itself could be understood as a symptom of wider socio-economic forces (the commoditization and alienation of the social by capitalism). Beckham's career seems exemplary in this regard: he is a good international level footballer, but the salary he commands, the media attention he receives and the global recognition level of his name and image are not commensurate with regard to his sporting ability. Moreover, Beckham "exemplifies indulgence in the consumer market" (Whannell 2002: 202): when stories appear about him in the media, they are more likely to have a business (Real Madrid marketing new Beckham gear in Asia), fashion (his latest haircut), gossip (stories about his relationship with his wife, or his affairs), pop culture (his autobiography) or lifestyle (Beckham the metrosexual) focus than be reporting something about his sporting activities. Football may have given him his initial entry point to media attention and fame, but largely because of his attraction to and ability to work the media, he is now firmly and even inextricably established in what Arjun Appadurai would call the commodity situation (1988: 13), where everything he says or does has exchange (within any number of media-related fields) as its primary or relevant function. Beckham is not just an example of the postmodern cliché about someone being famous for being famous: more specifically, he is an image-as-commodity that is exchangeable within just about any field at any place at any time.

To some extent Beckham, like Turgenev's superfluous man, is the embodiment of a time and a place – but the same could be said about any number of pop stars, writers, artists, television presenters, actors, squash players or international footballers, none of whom have achieved anything like Beckham's status. Any explication of the how and why of the Beckham phenomenon needs to take into account at least two more contexts: first, the trajectory of Beckham's career in English football, and second, the role of football in contemporary British culture, viewed within the still wider context of the changing socio-cultural functions and status of the field of sport. It is highly likely that David Beckham would have remained a relatively well-known English footballer – and not much more – if he had played the majority of his career with Aston Villa, Leeds United, Bolton Wanderers, Southampton or even Arsenal, Chelsea or Liverpool. Instead he played for Manchester United, which is the face of football for many people (particularly for those who have a relatively superficial familiarity with or interest in sport) in England and worldwide. There are various reasons why United occupies this place, the most obvious dating back to the Munich air disaster of 1958, when the team lost most of its players and was consequently 'taken on' by media and sympathetic football fans. It is arguable that the extraordinary non-footballing media attention given to George Best and Eric Cantona, for instance, not only prepared the way for Beckham – it made him necessary. In a sense the capital Beckham accumulated and the attention and status he received within the field of sport (including his elevation to the England captaincy and his multi-million pound transfer to Real Madrid, which substantially increased his status and value outside the field) owed a great deal to his original identification with the Manchester United football club – as Alex Ferguson implied at the time of his transfer to Real Madrid.

The second context we need to look at is the role of football in English culture. Raymond Boyle and Richard Haynes (1998) identify a number of factors dating from the 1980s, including the Heysel Stadium riot, the Hillsborough disaster, the relative success of the England team in the World Cup and European Championship, increased television coverage, and all-seater stadiums, as catalysts for attracting a wider demographic (affluent, professional, middle to upper middle class, younger, female) to the game. They particularly point to the role of media magnates (such as Rupert Murdoch, who has promoted the Premier League on BSkyB and in his newspapers) as having been crucial, in the words of an editorial from *The European* newspaper, "in transforming football, previously viewed as a 'slum sport'" into what it refers to as "the common currency of popular European culture" (1998: 34). This increased demographic supporter base for, and the enhanced coverage given to, football in Britain have been matched by similar trends with regard to other sports: rugby union, Olympic sports, cricket, Formula 1, snooker, horseracing, darts and rowing have increased their media coverage and attracted larger and more diversified audiences. This has produced a flow-on effect, with sporting teams and stars becoming more portable, appearing regularly in other areas of the media (soaps, reality television shows, celebrity interviews, advertising), which in turn raises the national profile of sport and its stars.

Beckham has been the most obvious beneficiary of these changes. But his emergence as sports star, pop icon and general cultural commodity rolled into one doesn't constitute evidence of a neat, unmediated or necessary articulation between wider socio-cultural events and forces and the field of sport. We made the point that Beckham's connection with Manchester United was as least as important to his rise as his good looks, his wife's celebrity status, or his football ability. Moreover, other factors such as the increased popularity of football within the wider context of British sport, and the changing status of sport vis-à-vis other cultural activities and fields (such as the arts, pop music and film), helped 'make' Beckham, to some extent. In other words, Beckham-as-commodity has emerged, like 'Rudin', out of a configuration of fields and forces that are arbitrary and motivated, in Benveniste's sense of the terms (1971). They're arbitrary because any player (Michael Owen rather than Beckham) and sport (tennis or boxing or athletics) or any field (art, pop music) could theoretically have filled the same structural function within the wider socio-cultural field. They're motivated because the outcomes were the result of a particular set of logics, imperatives and alignments of power: the ascendancy of the media and capitalism meant that, for reasons such as Beckham's Manchester United connection and pop star wife and the relatively low costs associated with programming sport in the media, Beckham and football were 'chosen' in advance.

CONCLUSION

To this point we have suggested that what we understand by sport and its activities (what is defined or categorized as sport, what are its socio-cultural functions) are necessarily the product of two closely related contexts – the internal dynamics of sport considered as a cultural field, and the vicissitudes that characterize the relation between sport and other cultural fields, including the wider social field. In our next chapter we will describe in detail the contexts and processes that gave rise, in nineteenth-century England, to the development of modern sport as a distinct ethos, set of activities, and cultural field.

3 Intimations of Sport

INTRODUCTION

We pointed out in our previous chapter that certain outdoor games have survived, in relatively similar forms, from ancient times. Although the evidence is often scanty and decontextualized (scenes painted on fragments of pottery, references from literary texts, wall paintings and artefacts from tombs), representations of activities that resemble bull fighting, wrestling, boxing, fencing, rowing, hunting, running, horseracing, swimming, polo, archery and games similar to golf and football have been found by archaeologists at Sumerian, Egyptian, Minoan, Assyrian, Greek, Etruscan, Roman, Harappan and Chinese sites. Consider Richard Mandell's description and interpretation of scenes found in an Egyptian tomb that were painted over four thousand years ago:

> One completed fresco ... from a tomb of a prince of the eleventh dynasty (2100–2000 B.C.) shows two wrestlers demonstrating 122 different positions and holds ... That these sports were already formal ... is shown by the lack of gouging and the absence of referees who would be necessary to impose the decorum essential for a combat to be maintained as a sport and not in earnest. That wrestling was so highly regarded as to be pursued by some professionals is suggested by a fresco dating from some six hundred years later, showing a marching group of stocky light-heavyweight wrestlers in loincloths. The last of their number carries a small standard upon which is the picture of a wrestler – the symbol of their trade. (1984: 21)

Leaving aside the leap of faith that is required in order to interpret representations of events and activities read four thousand years removed from the time/place of practice, there are two clear points of connection between Egyptian wrestling and modern sport. The first is at the level of technique: although we don't know what rules applied, the holds resemble those found in contemporary wrestling or cognate sports such as sumo wrestling (Baker 1982:9). Second, the high number of holds represented and the likelihood that the wrestlers had acquired professional or guild status suggest that the activities were characterized by specialization and some degree of uniformity and (perhaps verbal) codification: somebody was aware of, able to differentiate, and thought it important enough to record the one hundred and twenty-two different positions and holds that were available to, and practised by, wrestlers.

We can speculate about the social functions of these activities, and suggest that they served, among other things, as an extension of religious and/or political ceremonies or regimes; a form of recreation and entertainment; an adjunct to military training; and as a means of signalling and embodying class or caste differentiation. There is no evidence, however, that they constituted a distinct field of activity within Egyptian culture analogous to what we mean by sport. Most sport theorists and historians agree that what we understand as modern sport emerged in England sometime between the late eighteenth and mid-nineteenth centuries, and that its emergence was influenced by a variety of (interdependent) factors including changes in politics (parliamentarization, democracy and the rise of the middle class), demographics (urbanization, large cities), technology and communications (the telegraph, the railroads, industrialization), and society and culture (a mania for gambling, the increased influence of capitalism and consumerism, Elias' 'civilizing process'). None of these factors were present in ancient Egypt; nor was there a comparable sporting ethos promulgated by and inculcated within secondary and tertiary educational institutions, large crowds affiliated with teams from specific physical locations (urban centres, towns, cities or counties), widespread textual mediation (newspaper reports, scorecards and statistics) or influential institutional bodies that determined dates, rules and categories of play (the MCC, the English FA). And despite the relative wealth of evidence of what Mandell "loosely (calls) ... sport in Egyptian life" (1984:27), he is unwilling to make anything more than the following modest extrapolation:

> Until proven wrong we might well assume that if a society provides leisure, some stability, and the materials to work with, the people in that society will run, leap, climb, swim, wrestle and play ball. Furthermore we might assume that there will be informal as well as ceremonial competitions in these activities. It may not be hazardous to assume also that 'standing' or prestige was to be gained or lost in many or most cultures by the public demonstration of superiority in these skills. (27)

This characterization can be applied to most of the activities collected in Mandell's *Sport, a Cultural History* (1984) under the designation

'Sport Before the Greeks' (it is simply 'Before the Greeks' in Guttmann's *Sports Spectators* (1986). Egyptian games – or at least the representations we have of them – seem to have a stronger familial resemblance to modern sport than other ancient cultures. It is sufficiently strong enough for Mandell to write that it is "tempting to conclude that the Egyptians were the most athletic people before our times" (1984: 27), and for William Baker (1982) to characterize their depictions of fencing and other combat activities as having "the flavour of a contest that went beyond the bounds of religious ceremony" (8). But to some extent this is a product of the relative plenitude of archaeological evidence available in Egypt (as opposed to the dearth of evidence, say, from Harappan or Chinese sources). It is unlikely that the Egyptians were the only pre-Greek ancient culture characterized by a strong disposition to institutionalize games and athletic activities: although the evidence is paltry, we know that the pre-Tang Dynasty Chinese incorporated polo and archery into military training regimes, played a form of football, and developed and codified a game that bears a resemblance to golf (Mandell 1984). But any serious consideration of the intimation of modern sport must begin with the Greeks, for two main reasons. First, they developed a form of sports bureaucracy, a regime of rationalization and specialization, and an ethos of sport that provides what Allen Guttmann refers to as "intimations of the modern" (1978: 45). Second, and perhaps even more significantly, the modern cultural field of sport, both through its various official discourses and in a multitude of other texts (marketing and advertising, media reports, popular cultural representations of sport), consistently and self-consciously traces its origins back to the Greeks, and most particularly to the contests and ethos associated with the ancient Olympic Games.

GREEK ATHLETICS

Despite this strong discursive connection, Greek athletics festivals such as the Olympic Games don't match up particularly well with the seven features of modern sport (secularism, equality, specialization, bureaucratization, rationalization, quantification, records) outlined by Guttmann (1978). The four major athletic games or festivals (held every fourth year at Olympia, and in alternate years at Nemea, Isthmia and Delphi) had strong religious lineages, functions and affiliations: they were dedicated and sacred to different gods (Zeus, Apollo, Poseidon and Zeus again, respectively), and as Mark Golden observes, the Greeks themselves "located the origin of the Olympic Games squarely in the sphere of the divine" (1998: 14). Greek athletics evolved out of, and never entirely ceded its affiliations with, religious institutions and functions:

> Greek religion was essentially a matter of acts – rituals such as processions, sacrifices, feasts – not of creeds or dogmas. It might be argued that festivals, which brought together most of the acts characterizing Greek religion, were its most important public manifestation. By this token, athletic and equestrian competition, allied as it was with festival celebration, was intrinsically religious ... the association of athletics with religion was harmonious and lasting. At Olympia athletics came under religious supervision and took on religious overtones with sacred oaths, truces, prayers and dedications. (Golden 1998: 14–15)

There are other points of difference, such as the exclusion of barbarians (that is, non-Greeks), as well as women, slaves and non-adults (Golden 1998: 5). But where the ancient Greeks show the least affinity with modernity is in regard to standardization, quantification and record keeping. Guttmann makes the point that "modern sports are characterized by the almost inevitable tendency to transform every athletic feat into one that can be quantified and measured" (1978: 47), a situation that can be traced back to the more general tendency, which first appeared in the West in the seventeenth century (Mattelart 2003), to use mathematical models and forms of calculation in order to explicate or discover what was truthful, normal, reasonable and significant. It is not a matter of coincidence that the period which saw the emergence of modern sport was also characterized by the development of the positivist sciences (Saint-Simon, Comte), the earliest computer (Babbage's 'information machines'), statistics as a field of study and application (Quetelet), Taylorism and more generally "Sciences based on the calculation of individual behaviour" (Mattelart 2003: 37). As Guttmann observes: "We live in a world of numbers. The Greeks did not" (1978: 49). There were few records kept of distances covered by jumpers or times recorded by the runners, and when they are available they lack credibility – much like Herodotus' accounts of the numbers who took part in ancient battles. Moreover, there were no standard weights or dimensions for equipment, no times recorded, and in general very little quantification of practices apart from the number of victories ascribed to certain outstanding competitors. The imperative to set or break records, so central to our understanding and experience of many sporting contests, was unthinkable to the Greeks, precisely because in most instances there were no records to break.

Greek athletics was characterized by bureaucratization, rationalization and specialization, but only to a limited extent. Modern sport is a cultural field with its own bureaucratic structures that regulate, categorize, authorize and define everything that 'is the case'; in other words, they decide what belongs within the field. Institutions and their members also produce scientific research about training methods, analysis of tactical innovations, and arguments about rule changes, all of which are designed to bring about or facilitate improvements in sporting practices. Finally the field, and every sport and institution within it, is characterized by very specific categories and genres, including professionals and amateurs; sports doctors, masseurs, physios and psychologists; managers, trainers and coaches; and quarterbacks, wide receivers, tight ends and running backs. Now consider Richard Mandell's description of the athletic festival at Olympia in the fifth century:

> The festival was well prepared. Every fourth year in the spring three heralds set out from Elis on routes that covered the entire Greek world. As they arrived at each polis or colony they proclaimed a sacred Olympic truce. Thereafter competitors and spectators traveling to or from Olympia were under the protection of Zeus. They dared not bare arms, nor could they be attacked by armed men. There were only a few violations of the truce during the many centuries of Olympia's fame. Competitors with their trainers and provisions might arrive months before the festival actually began. Once at Olympia, the athletes were under the supervision of the Elian judges, who had to ascertain the athlete's eligibility. They had to be sure that every competitor was a citizen of pure Greek ancestry and had to decide if a youth might be too old to be included in the boy's events and therefore compete as a man ... the sites of the sporting events were overgrown and needed to be cleared of weeds and debris. The stadium had to be covered with a layer of fresh sand. (1984: 46)

The organization of the Olympic festival every four years (not to mention the other important festivals at Nemea, Isthmia and Delphi every second year, and those one-offs held in honour of and in conjunction with the funerals of private citizens) required a bureaucracy of some kind, even if it was part-time (it might come into being prior to or for the duration of events), discontinuous (one set of elected officials taking the place of another) and predominantly oral in its textualizing or disseminating of information (although rule books and training manuals were available). To put things in perspective, the festival at Olympia dates from at least 776 BC, and continued, in various forms, until it was banned by the Byzantine Emperor Theodosius at the end of the fourth century AD – a span of almost twelve hundred years. It involved competitors and spectators not just from Greece but also from the wider Greek world (including Sicily, Southern Italy and parts of Asia) and eventually from across the Roman Empire. And the games – and Greek athletics in general – involved considerably more than the already relatively complex logistics (the movement of heralds and competitors, the vetting of athletes, the preparation of the stadium) outlined above. Every major polis had its own gymnasium and wrestling school which contributed to the institutionalizing of Greek sport (Mandell 1984: 71), and towards the end of the fifth century BC a kind of athletics circuit was in place, characterized by substantial prize money, competition between cities to attract athletes, specialization, professionalism, coaching and even private masseurs and cooks (Mandell 1984: 70). McIntosh describes such athletes as "pot hunters" who were remunerated as "full-time specialist entertainers" (1987: 22–3), and argues that by this time the "appellation athlete was no longer a badge of honour but was a label of a special class who dieted and trained for their careers in such a way as to set them apart from ordinary citizens" (22–3). But Greek athletic bureaucracy, even after the fifth century, was essentially part-time, contingent and derived from other areas of activity (such as religion). And Guttmann points out that even when that bureaucracy was extended, stabilized and secularized under the Romans, it never approached the "ubiquity of ... administrative forms" (1978: 46) that characterizes modern sport. Nor was there any equivalent in Greek or Roman institutional practices comparable to the level of standardization achieved by the Marylebone Cricket Club in England as early as the nineteenth century, which prescribed and enforced "precise regulations for the weight of the ball, the width of the bat, the distance between wickets, the dimensions of the wicket, etc." (Guttmann 1978: 46).

The most significant connection between Greek athletics and modern sport occurs at the level of the idea, or perhaps more specifically, at the level of discourse. For the Greeks' athletic activity had a value that was not reducible to mere utility – for instance simply as a form of training for war (although it clearly served this purpose, particularly in Sparta, and continued to do so even after the advent of professionalism). Various suggestions have been made as to how best to articulate this sense of value, but they can perhaps be collected under the general rubrics of religion; cultural, social and political differentiation; and the body. The religious dimension is straightforward enough: to partake in athletic festivals was associated with honouring the gods, and to win an event was meant to signal divine favour or portend good fortune for the individual and his community. In certain cases it resulted in the deification of the winner (Mandell 1984: 48). Similarly there can be little doubt about the role of athletics as a means of differentiating identities within Greek society and culture, as Mark Golden (1998) makes clear: non-Greeks were originally barred from competing, as were slaves, women and non-adults; victory brought considerable capital both to individuals and their communities; to be able to put teams into competition in the equestrian events denoted class and wealth; and the politician Alcibiades spent huge sums of money in order to win the Olympic four-horse chariot race in 416 BC and thereby improve his political fortunes (173).

The value and function of the body is a more complex issue: it is imbricated with the wider Greek idea of society as a (potentially) "balanced, harmonious, united human group", and of social relations as (ideally) rational and geometrical (Vernant 1990: 95). The body is both one important site of the manifestation of that harmony and balance, and also a medium of learning how to achieve it (Foucault 1980: 61): in other words, it has a political, aesthetic and a pedagogical value and function. Consider the following passage from Mandell regarding Greek spectators and their appreciation of athletic bodies:

> The graceful motion under full power of the big athletes who specialized in the field events often roused the massed spectators to raptures of admiration. The accomplished, honor-laden pentathlon athlete was the one most likely to be watched and sketched by artists. The artists were attempting ... in their depiction of the moving male body to establish canons of human beauty. (1984: 50)

The canons of beauty he refers to here don't arise from consideration of material form of and for itself; on the contrary, that physical form is beautiful and admirable only to the extent that it constitutes an embodiment of the idea of moderation, balance, harmony and grace revealed and articulated as a history or story of (a successful) struggle. The pentathlete is particularly admirable because the struggle is far greater and more demanding – the body must adjust to and learn to overcome a variety of challenges and impediments. From this perspective, athletic contests are struggles with a definite pedagogical function: the athlete learns not only from agonistics with other competitors, but also competes to learn to overcome the limitations or flaws (both physical and mental) that characterize the self.

The relation between Greek athletics and modern sport is often represented as ideals that helped precipitate, and continue to be identified with, the revived Olympic Games; this connection derived from a more general revival of interest in Greek thought and culture in Europe in the eighteenth and nineteenth centuries, strongly associated with romanticism and intellectual figures such as Goethe, Schlegel, Schiller, Nietzsche and Pater. It influenced the field of sport as early as the first part of the nineteenth century, contributing to the development of the *Turnen* gymnastics movement in Germany and to the institutionalizing of games in English public schools. Most sports analysts and historians refer to Baron Charles de Coubertin's desire to revive the original festival of Olympia as being fundamental to the staging of the first modern Olympic Games in Athens in 1896, but Coubertin's zeal also owed much to the example of early nineteenth-century English public school appropriation of the ideals, functions and ethos of Greek athletics, and in particular to the supposed relationship between agonistics, learning and character. Guttmann (1992) refers to de Coubertin's reverential pilgrimage to the chapel at Thomas Arnold's Rugby School and the influence it exerted on him in the following terms:

> Coubertin, like a number of other anglophile Frenchmen, admired the rugged health of the English schoolboys. Sport seemed, moreover, to have developed not only the boys' enviable physical prowess but also their character. They glowed with a sturdy self-confidence that their teachers – most of whom were sports enthusiasts – attributed to their hours at cricket, soccer, and rugby. Although the Duke of Wellington never did remark that the Battle of Waterloo was won on the playing fields of Eton, generations of Englishmen believed in a vital connection between sports and life's more serious contests. Coubertin shared that belief. He was as sure as they were that that character developed in schoolboy games manifested itself in firm British rule over 'an empire upon which the sun never set'. (1992: 9)

Coubertin is a particularly useful point of reference here, since the curious contradictions that are symptomatic of modern sport's relation to its Greek heritage are central to the reasons and motivations behind his appropriation of Greek and English public school athletics. Coubertin, "shaken by the class divisions that threatened to destroy French society, dedicated his life to the restoration of social peace and domestic harmony" (Guttmann 1992: 7); but he countenanced an Olympic movement predicated on the doctrine of amateurism, which effectively excluded the non-amateur lower classes. He was also a fervent nationalist "haunted by the memories of the Franco-Prussian War", the French defeat of which he attributed to "the physical inferiority of the average French youth" (Guttmann 1992: 8); at the same time he was an internationalist who wanted the modern Olympics to play a role in overcoming international divisions and misunderstandings. For Coubertin all these aims could be achieved – and such contradictions resolved – via the example of Greek athletics, reincarnated as the ethos of modern sport. The struggle of the individual gave rise to a fraternity predicated on mutual adherence and commitment to respecting the rules and spirit of the game; in short, to struggle against the other – whether at the level of classes or nations – was to dissolve the differences, antagonisms and misunderstandings that are constitutive of otherness.

ROMAN GAMES

The profound discursive influence exercised on the field of sport by Greek athletics can be contrasted with the massive neglect of Roman athletics and games, despite their very obvious affinities with the twentieth-century experience of sport-as-spectacle. As Guttmann remarks, we "celebrate our Olympics and imagine ourselves the heirs of ancient Hellas, but we are probably closer ... to the howling crowds of 'Blues' and 'Greens' that cheered on the charioteers of Constantinople" (1978: 50). There are few similarities between Greek and Roman attitudes to and practices of athletics, despite the Roman appropriation of Greek athletic festivals and culture in the middle of the second century BC. While some emperors showed an enthusiasm for and an admiration of Greek athletics, and wealthy citizens (most notably the legendary Herodes Atticus) helped finance and revive Olympia and other festivals, by and large Rome remained unconvinced and unconverted:

> The athletic movement initiated by Augustus was, at least as far as Italy was concerned, purely artificial. The athletic festival was to the Romans nothing more than a show. In the first century of our era they still regarded the Greeks with a certain contempt, and despised Greek athletics. To strip naked and to contend in public was degrading in the eyes of a Roman citizen. (Gardiner 1930: 49)

The Romans differed from the Greeks in their attitude to games, which they viewed as a form of popular entertainment designed to amuse (and in some cases, divert or assuage the disaffections or discontents of) the people. Gladiatorial contests filled the fifty thousand capacity Colosseum, and the chariot races in the Hippodrome in Rome and Constantinople attracted as many as two hundred and fifty thousand spectators at a time (Guttmann 1986: 28). We would certainly recognize Mandell's following account of Roman chariot racing as quintessentially modern:

> In the capital ... the popularity of chariot racing led to professional associations of drivers. Rival stables attracted fanatical and antagonistic allegiances. The colours of the blouses worn by drivers had taken on symbolic though ephemeral meanings by the first century AD. We read in the records about the fans of the Reds, the Whites, the Golds, and the Purples. But two rivals were most persistent: the Blues and the Greens ... Rival politicians, mutually damning religious sects, feuding clans, or antagonistic classes, might attach their loyalty to one color or shift to another. This ... rivalry led to bribery and riots that regularly disrupted urban life. Sometimes famous drivers or whole stables would abandon their traditional color to adopt that of their erstwhile enemies ... These intense ... allegiances became aspects of Roman public life that reached far beyond the race course and outlasted Rome itself. (1984: 81)

The popularity and continuity of the Roman games gave rise to a level of professionalism, specialization and bureaucratization that, along with their strongly secular nature, enables them to match up quite well with

Guttmann's seven features of modern sport (1978). And to some extent the Roman concept of spectatorship, the bureaucratic transformation of athletics into a form of entertainment, and the culture of mass identification with athletes and teams is as close to modern sport as anything derived from Greece.

The Roman and Byzantine phenomenon of the mass spectator affiliation with chariot racing teams, represented by colours (usually the Reds, Whites, Blues and Greens) is of particular relevance here, since regardless of how the field of sport produces and articulates itself within an idealized discourse of fairness and equality, pedagogy, character building, play, skill and aesthetics, one of the defining characteristics of contemporary sport-as-practice is the relationship between teams and supporters or fans. As Guttmann points out, this aspect of sport has often been reduced to questions of "the problems of sports-related violence and the measures taken to control it" (1986: 2). The political and social functions of spectatorship, however, are a complex and significant issue, one that can't be exhausted by debates about the extent to which sports spectatorship facilitates or compromises Elias' notion of sport as part of a wider 'civilizing process'. Spectatorial identification is clearly tied in with processes and notions of communal and collective identity, but what is most interesting about the Roman and Byzantine affiliations with racing team colours is the abstracted nature of that identification. Although there are debates about the extent to which chariot races had specific political functions (see Guttmann 1986 and Cameron 1976), it does seem that these forms of identification had no obvious or enduring geographical, class or political inflection; in other words, the colours were, in Claude Lefort's terms (Lefort 1986), 'empty signifiers' which different groups from Rome and Byzantium more or less 'filled in' as they went along. At the same time this form of identification was capable of arousing extraordinary attachments, passion and violence:

> In Constantinople, the circus factions ... set the city's wooden hippodrome on fire in 491, 498, 507, and 532 AD, after which Justinian prudently invested in a marble stadium. In the fifth and sixth centuries, spectator violence in the Byzantine Empire increased to the point where troops were repeatedly called upon to restore order. After a victory by Porphyrius in 507 in the circus at Antioch, the jubilant Greens ran wild and, in the course of the riot, burned the local synagogue, a quite typical instance of anti-Semitism. The worst of these many riots took place in Constantinople in January 532 when supporters of both the Blues and the Greens joined forces. Prisoners about to be executed ... were rescued by the mob, which subsequently ignored Justinian's attempt to appease them with the promise of additional games ... the unpacified mob proclaimed a new emperor to whom a number of senators paid homage. Fortunately for Justinian, his most skilful general, Belisarius, arrived in time to save the day – at the cost of an estimated 30,000 lives. (Guttmann 1986: 32)

Probably the main reason that this Roman legacy never achieved the discursive status of Greek athletics is because when the field of sport was developing in the nineteenth century, it acquired a significant (upper) class inflection which was far more receptive to the idea of a stylized and aestheticized agonistics (with its distinctive combination of disinterestedness and/as utility) than it was to what Guttmann, following Gibbon, refers to as the "barbarizing process" (1986: 34) of the violent, bloodthirsty and populist Roman games. With the fall of Rome in the fifth century AD the thoroughly modern set of institutions, apparatuses, bureaucracies, events and dispositions didn't entirely disappear with it: the Roman passion for chariot races "thrived as a form of political ceremony, factional rivalry, and public entertainment well into the Middle Ages, possibly as late as the twelfth century" (Baker 1982: 40). In post-Roman Europe, however, games and athletic competitions largely reverted to a localized and relatively unorganized set of activities of the kind that pre-dated Greece and Rome.

THE EUROPEAN MIDDLE AGES AND THE RENAISSANCE

This didn't mean that in the medieval world games ceased to be played, either widely or in a multiplicity of forms, or that no connections can be made between the Middle Ages and contemporary sport. If Greek athletics gave sport its ideals and values, and Roman games presaged its bureaucratic and spectatorial nature, the Middle Ages provided it with a significant part of its content:

> During the Middle Ages ... Roman frontier games and Islamic cultic rituals combined with native European customs to provide a richly varied pattern of popular pastimes. The dominant institution of the period, the Catholic Church, adapted various 'pagan' rites for Christian worship. Many of these ceremonies featured a symbolic tossing of a ball back and forth as a dramatic representation of the struggle between good and evil. Playful dramatization soon leaped the bounds of their religious origins. As the Church provided seasonal holidays and physical sites for play, ball games flourished in Medieval Europe. By the twelfth century, peasants enjoyed numerous types of handball, football, and stick-and-ball games. No written rules existed; each game evolved differently from one place to another according to local custom and whim. But in the play of Medieval peasants lay the roots of virtually every ball game known in the modern world. (Baker 1982: 42)

By and large these activities bore very little resemblance to popular contemporary ball games such as football, cricket, baseball, golf and hockey. They were usually a capricious amalgam of the above, played without hard and fast rules on and across whatever grounds and territories (and waterways) were at hand for as long as people remained interested, and without regard to most of the categories, distinctions, imperatives and equipment that characterizes their modern relatives. Games were regularly played between or within villages or local regions on feast days under the patronage of the church, but apart from these continuities they were distinctly 'of the moment'. There were no referees, and the numbers participating ebbed and flowed. No distinction was made between spectators and players; men, women, adolescents and children competed against each other; and violence (including the use of knives) was endemic, to the extent that the most popular precursor of football, called kicking-camp or camp-ball, was frequently legislated against and outlawed in the thirteenth and fourteenth centuries (McLean 1983).

Apart from providing the forerunners of football and other ball games, medieval Europe's main link with modern sport is to be found in the aristocratic tournaments, tilts and jousts that probably originated in Germany in the ninth century (Carter 1992), and achieved a level of organizational sophistication and complexity, not to mention what we could call an international dimension (McLean 1983). By the sixteenth century these once "crude tournaments" (McLean 1983: 62) which were largely predicated on specific and very serious utilities (as preparation, training or substitutes for war), and which sometimes were the occasion of greater fatalities and casualties than real battles, had become "artistic performances as well as chivalrous games and political meetings" (McLean 1983: 62). The refined tournaments and jousts of the fourteenth century onward are useful case studies with regard to the application of the civilizing process (in the Eliasian sense) to games – and for the analysis and evaluation of that applicability. The discourses, rules, values and imperatives of chivalry certainly applied a restraining hold on and over, and gave a kind of ethical shape to, what had been little more than melees.

Tournaments and jousts can be read both as exemplifications, and simulations, of a civilizing process; what is undeniable, however, is the extent to which, during the transition from the medieval to the Renaissance period and beyond, they constitute a re-emergence of games as popular entertainment and spectacle. Part fashion-show and part charade, tournaments and jousts turned into simulations of war without any obvious military utility. As Cashmore and other commentators make clear, they became increasingly 'of and for themselves', while acquiring a spectatorial inflection similar to that of the Roman and Byzantine circuses:

> After the sixteenth century, the grand tournaments faded and rural events emerged, though tilts were often at targets ... The process is familiar to anyone

who has witnessed the transmutation of wrestling after it became a popular spectator 'sport'. (Cashmore 1990: 52)

Cashmore's reference to professional wrestling is not misguided: as Teresa McLean makes clear, tilts and tournaments increasingly removed themselves from any connection with their objects of representation (battles and personal combat between knights, tests of strength and courage). The mock-combatants, who often attacked targets rather than human adversaries, were increasingly drawn from the non-aristocratic classes; equipment took on the status of theatrical props rather than weapons, and the rituals, categories and subjectivities associated with the tournament merged with, or were incorporated into, quite different social genres:

> The only contest in the tilt-yard that could be linked with the old tradition of the tourney was provided by the groom and guests at a wedding, which had been elevated into grand pageantry for the amusement of the spectators, a parody of the knightly chivalries and an indication perhaps, that Tudor England was about to enter a great age of theatrical entertainment and expression. (McLean 1983: 27)

As tilts and tourneys became increasingly subject to the imperative to entertain, the (eventual) presence of non-aristocratic urban crowds and the burgeoning size of the events demanded a complex level of organization, involving months and in some cases years of preparation (Guttmann 1986: 38). Of course this emphasis on what Guttmann would refer to as the 'modern' aspect of Tudor and Elizabethan games, or even the drawing of analogies with Rome and Byzantium, need to be kept in perspective: Europe at this time had no cities of comparable size to ancient Rome, crowds usually numbered in the low thousands (Guttmann 1986: 35), and there wasn't to be the development of Roman-style professional apparatuses until well into the nineteenth century. And yet the fact that tournaments and the like went from being entirely participatory to predominantly spectatorial events constitutes one important example of post-Roman games and physical activities presaging modern sport.

Another significant development in Renaissance Europe and England that impacted upon the culture of games and physical activities was the ethos and discourses of 'humanism' which, following the example of classical Greece, incorporated a consideration of the body into pedagogical regimes. The importance that came to be ascribed to physical education was partly derived from the work of a number of Italian and European scholars, most particularly Castiglione's *The Book of the Courtier* (Brailsford 1969). Castiglione's idealized 'Renaissance Man' was equally at home fighting, at court, in wider society, competing in games and appreciating and practising the arts. Physical activity was one important manifestation of cultural training, understood an unproblematical amalgam of utility (an occasion of training both for war and wider social duties) and disinterestedness (an effortless, stylized and aestheticized activity practised of and for itself). While the general populace mainly amused themselves with blood sports such as cock-fighting and bull- and bear-baiting, gentlemen engaged in more or less sanctioned activities such as hunting, running, wrestling, swimming, archery, fencing, handball and bowls, and university students and (upper class) schoolchildren played popular sports such as camp-ball and versions of cricket as part of their physical education curriculum. These physical activities were part of a regime that was theoretically rational, and which trained and disposed both the mind and the body with regard to certain specified ends (which included more 'moral' or 'civilized' virtues such as restraint, temperance, grace, decency, reason and modesty, as well as military prowess).

If all this sounds remarkably familiar it is because it both looks back to the Greeks and simultaneously anticipates – and in a sense provides the blueprint for the development, four hundred years later, of – the ethos associated with English public school games and the concept of amateurism. But as Brailsford points out, it also sets in train a logic of institutionalization, bureaucratization, standardization and just about every other marker or characteristic of sport as a (modern) cultural field:

> Essential to the exercise of the courtier was the sense of style in his games playing: a victory was sweet, but graceful defeat was preferable to a fashionless triumph. It would be too much to ascribe phrases such as 'a good loser', 'the game's what matters, not the result', and the aesthetic attitudes which give us 'a glorious cover drive' and even 'a beautiful left jab' wholly to the courtly tradition: they are modified and conditioned by many later overloadings ... from the playing ethos of the late nineteenth and twentieth century public schools. Yet some of their inspiration lies in this Renaissance style of exercise, which flourished for the formative hundred years or more when games and sporting activities were, for almost the first time, being subjected to a deliberate and conscious intellectual scrutiny. Out of this conscious evaluation, and as a concomitant of the courtly demand for formal style, developed a respect for rules within which play could achieve a desirable regularity ... Rules developed in complexity and formality ... and they often demanded an arbiter or referee ... To the Renaissance courtly tradition can thus be attributed the origins of both the moral and character-building claims that have been frequently made for sports and games in later days. (1969: 81–2)

The influence of Humanism and the Courtly tradition quickly waned in England, but, if anything, recreational and physical activities assumed an even greater significance: during the seventeenth century games and rituals were the objects of frequent sectarian and monarchical interests and inter-vention, and certain activities (particularly horseracing) developed into highly organized and professionalized forms of popular entertainment. While the Puritans denounced and banned blood sports and demonstrated a suspicion of all things pleasurable and bodily, the Stuarts championed the culture of 'merry old England' – which ensured that physical activities and pastimes remained highly politicized affairs. James I rescinded the ban on many recreational activities, and was a would-be athlete and games enthu-siast who established Newmarket as the centre of the English racing indus-try; and Charles I sanctioned Sunday games through the issue of a Royal Edict. Royal patronage resumed with the Restoration. Charles II, as well as taking an interest in tennis as a participant, was "an arbiter of sporting practices" (Brailsford 1969: 212) who codified and standardized bowls and racing, and ruled on racing wagers; and James II was an "enthusiastic yachtsman" (Baker 1982: 87), who owned racehorses and sanctioned the introduction of professional jockeys. Nor did this patronage cease with the Glorious Revolution: William III frequently attended, entered horses in, and bet heavily on, the races; and Queen Anne "left her mark as a shrewd, busi-nesslike owner, adding the famous Darley Arabian breed to the Godolphin Arabian and Byerly Turk stock and laying the foundations for the Royal Ascot, a course destined to be the most fashionable in the world" (Baker 1982: 88).

THE PRE-MODERN PERIOD

The seventeenth and eighteenth centuries saw the "formulation ... (of) a number of sophisticated, 'modern' sports" (Brailsford 1969: 214) – and more importantly, some of the core markers (professionalism, standardiza-tion of rules, governing bodies, organizational bureaucracies, rationaliza-tion and specialization of roles and equipment, fixture dates or lists) of sport as a distinctive cultural field. The main stimulus for this development was not the civilizing process, demographics, technological change, the advent of cap-italism, the ideas and ideals of physical improvement, or political pro-grammes. Rather it was due, as Brailsford makes clear, to the increase in the number and size of the wagers made on incipient sports such as racquets, hand ball, bowls, cricket, boxing, wrestling, rowing and most particularly racing:

> Betting increased considerably and the stakes grew higher and higher, until, in
> 1698, William III was staking 2,000 guineas on his horse matched against the

Duke of Somerset. With such heavy, financial involvements, sports obviously had to be regulated; and racing provides another example of the pattern seen already in cricket and repeated, almost without exception, in other sports: rules were first drawn up for individual competitions or matches, and later extended to become the rules of the game itself. It is sobering to consider that the regulation of games grew up not from noble motives of 'fair play', or even merely out of a desire for tidiness, but to protect the financial interests of gamblers. (1969: 213)

The decline in royal involvement and interest in racing and other outdoor activities and entertainments in the Georgian period was more than compensated for by an increase in aristocratic patronage and entrepreneurial activity, and a concomitant acceleration in the formalization of rules, methods of arbitration and standards of play. William Baker characterizes this period and its activities in terms of the rubric 'The Quest for Order' (1982: 88). In horseracing the Jockey Club was formed in 1750 and the first Racing Calendar published in 1770; cricket umpires started officiating in the early seventeen hundreds, and various sets of rules were developed, most significantly by the Duke of Richmond in 1729, the 'Cricket Club' in 1744, and by the MCC in 1787. Similar trends could be found in other sports, notably boxing, which although illegal during most of the second half of the eighteenth century, still attracted large crowds and managed to differentiate itself from other popular forms of combat by carefully designating how, where and under what circumstances opponents could be assaulted.

It is generally agreed that many of the features associated with modernity – the rise of new middle class with time and money on their hands, the pervasive socio-political influence of capitalism, changing demographics and the rise of urban centres, and advances in transport and communication, most particularly the popular press – provided an impetus to the development of sport in the nineteenth century. And yet all of these characteristics are to be found, to a greater or lesser extent, in the eighteenth century, along with another equally significant factor – an incipient mass culture:

The middle-class culture which ... (the) commercialisation of leisure brought about expanded greatly in the nineteenth century, modified maybe, but not essentially changed, and lasted until our own time ... In the early eighteenth century, culture and sport slowly ceased to be elitist and private and became increasingly public. The more public culture and sporting activity becomes, the more it provokes social emulation ... And social emulation usually leads to increasing consumption and expenditure. And it encourages the entrepreneur to exploit and extend this market. Furthermore, the media of communication of the eighteenth century ... all helped to diffuse, in a way never before experienced by Englishmen, social attitudes ... the seepage of ideas which is the distinguishing mark of leisure in western society. (Plumb 1974: 19)

Games were integrated into this regime of popular or mass leisure culture, but to widely differing extents. Horseracing was professionalized, highly organized, standardized and bureaucratized; attracted large crowds of spectators and gamblers from all classes; was truly national in scope; and because of its aristocratic capital and connections, had developed a kind of nexus with the emerging popular press – although the publication of results was slow (sometimes weeks after the event), and references to upcoming meetings depended on whether they were of significant social status and interest. The Jockey Club eventually produced its own publication, the *Racing Calendar*, which "allowed both the policing and capitalization of the racing programme. Any race not advertised in the Racing Calendar was not recognized by the ruling body, enabling a strict control of the sport's administration" (Boyle and Haynes 2000: 25).

The other great popular spectator games of the eighteenth century – boxing and cricket – were less co-ordinated and consistent in their development. The "first regular references to cricket matches appear after the Restoration" (Holt 1989: 25), but attempts at codification had to wait until the vogue for gambling on cricket and the involvement of aristocratic patrons such as the Duke of Richmond (who drew up the first rules of the game in 1727). In contrast to other games in the eighteenth century, cricket was integrated into the burgeoning mass culture market both at the level of national spectatorship (drawing crowds of up to ten thousand, and featuring teams drawn from and representing different regions of the country) and local participation (Holt refers to "a surprisingly dense network of village clubs, especially in the south and east of England") (1989: 27). However, the already fractious nature of the relations between various 'stakeholders' – aristocrats, entrepreneurs, and clubs – was accentuated by county rivalries and the class and 'north-south divide', which militated against the kind of administrative and legal control achieved by the Jockey Club with horseracing. As for boxing, the efforts of entrepreneurs such as James Figgis and Jack Broughton to codify the "manly art of self-defence" (Baker 1982: 91) were interrupted when it was made illegal in 1750, and while it continued to draw large crowds and attract the attention of journalists and the patronage of royalty and literary figures such as Byron and William Hazlitt, it had to wait until the nineteenth century before it was properly institutionalized.

Football (or camp-ball), on the other hand, remained an activity not overly removed from its medieval roots: its integration into rural festivals and urban guild rivalries still constituted its primary social significance in the eighteenth century. Richard Holt, drawing on Carew's *Survey of Cornwall* and his description of a game of 'hurling at goales', makes the point that:

These games were not just the contests of brute strength that they were assumed to have been by the inventors of 'new' games in the mid-nineteenth century. As the observer of the Norfolk game remarks, if the teams were well matched – and the idea of balancing up sides carefully in itself assumes a fairly sophisticated concept of play – the scoring of goals 'is no easy achievement, and often requires much time, many doublings, detours and exertions'. (1989: 14)

At the same time, and in contrast not just to horseracing, boxing and cricket but also to other popular activities such as wrestling, fencing, cudgelling and rowing, football essentially remained both a participatory and a localized game: its transformation into a national and international spectator sport (actually sports, since it takes on and is codified as disparate identities, including football, rugby union and league, Gaelic football, American football and Australian rules) had to wait until the remarkable shift in demographics and the development of mass modes of transportation and communication that accompanied the industrial revolution.

There are two other developments in games and physical activities in the eighteenth century that strongly presage modern sport. The first of these was the appearance, predominantly in schools in Germany and Central Europe, of highly organized regimes of drill, exercise and physical education (marching, gymnastics, walking, swimming, running) that are opposed to "Traditional children's games which, which encouraged spontaneity, fantasy, and useless fun" (Mandell 1984: 160). It gave rise, in the short term, to the German nationalistic Turnen movement, the Czech Sokol and the Jewish Maccabian organizations, and later to the incorporation of medical and physical sciences into government sponsored and funded sports programmes, most notably and comprehensively in Eastern Europe in the second half of the twentieth century.

The second development, also influenced by Enlightenment attitudes and ideas and very much in keeping with Elias' notion of the civilizing process, was the spread of organized and institutionalized opposition to traditional blood sports. In order to understand how this movement spread while cockfighting, bear-baiting, cudgelling, boxing and other related activities were proliferating and enjoying unparalleled popularity, we have to take up Plumb's point that "the media of communication of the eighteenth century ... all helped to diffuse, in a way never before experienced by Englishmen, social attitudes" (Plumb 1974: 19). Newspapers, magazines, pamphlets, novels and essays, the mouthpieces – and facilitators – of middle class standards of behaviour and morality, articulated the imperatives of and guidelines for what Elias would call a "regularity of conduct and sentiment" (Elias 1993: 151). Giving one's time over to, and deriving pleasure from, the agonies and torments suffered by animals and humans (at least in an overt way) gradually became a marker of the non-human, of the masses, and of deviancy. What we have in late eighteenth-century England is a situation whereby the increasing demand for blood spectacles and the willingness of entrepreneurs to provide them was matched and eventually (more or less) overturned, through the use of various legal, political, social and cultural mechanisms and interventions, by the imperatives and values of the 'civilizing process' – at least among the middle classes.

CONCLUSION

Richard Holt refers to the "two broad themes" that characterize English games before the Victorian period:

> Firstly, the importance of sports as an element in a festive culture that was orally transmitted and had a high customary tolerance for violent behaviour of all kinds along with a good deal of gambling, eating and drinking. This, if you like, was 'traditional' sport in the sense that the seasons, the 'holy days' of the church, the rites of apprenticeship, the patronage of the landed, and the customs of the locality were the determining factors of play. However there was a second level too. This was the more organized world of pugilism, rowing, racing and cricket where written rules were established, challenges were issued and advertised in the press, and large crowds gathered to watch and to wager ... Over-concentration on football, which was perhaps untypical in its relatively late regulation ... tends to obscure the degree to which sport was already evolving along more complex and commercial lines between the mid-eighteenth and mid-nineteenth centuries. (1989: 28)

In our next chapter we turn our attention to the various contexts and factors – social, cultural, technological, political and economic – that ushered in this evolution in England and the United States in the nineteenth century, and to the sites, processes and discourses that helped produce the ethos, idea and cultural field of modern sport.

4 The Field of Sport

INTRODUCTION

In *Homo Ludens* Johan Huizinga puts forward the proposition that the advent of modern sport, and concomitantly the beginning of the end of play, can be traced to a specific time and place. He describes this period and process as a transition:

> from occasional amusement to the system of organized clubs and matches ... The great ball-games in particular require the existence of permanent teams, and herein lies the starting-point of modern sport. The process arises quite spontaneously in the meeting of village against village, school against school, one part of the town against the rest. (1966: 196)

and goes on to outline the factors that helped bring about this development:

> That the process started in 19th-century England is understandable up to a point, though how far the specifically Anglo-Saxon bent of mind can be deemed an efficient cause is less certain. But it cannot be doubted that the structure of English social life had much to do with it. Local self-government encouraged the spirit of association ... The absence of obligatory military training favoured ... the need of ... physical exercise. The peculiar form of education tended to work in the same direction, and finally the geography of the country and the nature of the terrain ... were of the greatest importance. Thus England became the cradle and focus of modern sporting life. (197)

as well as some of the more significant consequences:

> Ever since the last quarter of the 19th century games, in the guise of sport, have been taken more and more seriously. The rules have become increasingly strict and elaborate. Records are established at a higher ... level than ever conceivable

before ... Now, with the increasing systematization and regimentation of sport, something of the pure play-quality is inevitably lost ... The spirit of the professional is no longer the true play-spirit; it is lacking in spontaneity and carelessness ... sport ... becomes a thing ... neither play nor earnest ... However important it may be for the players or spectators, it remains sterile. The old play-factor has undergone almost complete atrophy. (197–8)

The arguments articulated in *Homo Ludens* remain widely influential: leading sports historians such as Baker, Guttmann and Mandell all more or less accept the idea that what occurred in England in the nineteenth century constituted a paradigmatic shift of some kind. Explanations regarding the rise of the modern field of sport usually focus on a combination of social, historical, economic, political and technological factors that were specific to nineteenth-century England. The ones most frequently identified or attested to are the full integration of capitalism and capitalist values and imperatives into the wider social field; industrialization; urbanization; a burgeoning middle class; developments in transport and communication technology; the spread of literacy and the increase in and influence of popular newspapers and magazines; higher wages and increased leisure time; the spread of the British Empire and colonialism; a significant acceleration (facilitated by increasing legislative intervention) in the processes of sportization; and finally an institutionalizing, within the field of education and at the level both of discourse and practice, of the notion of sport as integral to regimes of pedagogy – with the concomitant assumption that such regimes would have much wider socio-political utilities and applications.

MODERNIZATION AND THE REASON OF STATE

At the beginning of the nineteenth century capitalist imperatives and forces brought about technological and scientific developments that paved the way for the industrialization of Britain, which in turn brought about a dramatic shift of the population from the countryside to cities such as London and Manchester. This concentration of populations in urban centres was accompanied by increased wages and leisure time among workers, and the spread of the middle-class, which increased the demand for mass cultural commodities and services (including sports competitions and goods) that had started to develop in the eighteenth century. More sophisticated transport and communication technology linked these industrial centres, which not only facilitated the flow of goods and industrial materials, but also opened the way for highly organized, professional, national and eventually international sporting bodies and competitions that required consistent codes, rules and fixtures. Finally, Britain's position as an imperial power (in fact the imperial power) enabled it to effect a kind of cultural colonization of the world, with sport in the vanguard: so Europe and South America took up association football, the Empire played cricket, and more generally the world (eventually) embraced the modern notion of sport. While these factors are usually seen as the catalyst for the development of contemporary sport, they were also inflected by the wider socio-political and cultural imperatives, logics and characteristics of modernization. Guttmann argues (1978) that secularism, democracy and equality, specialization, rationalization, bureaucratization and quantification gave rise to national and international governing bodies (such as the AAA, the FA, the IOC and FIFA); universally standardized rules, team numbers, distances and dimensions (of playing fields and equipment); and the concept of the records and the extension of support services (managers, physios, psychologists, skills coaches, and staff with scientific, sports medicine and dietary expertise). The concept of rationalization can be usefully related to the activities and techniques of what Foucault calls the 'reason of state', 'discursive regimes' and 'bio-power' (1997). He argues that in much of Europe from the eighteenth century on and particularly in the nineteenth century, the state's population came to be understood as a resource, and the proper role of the state as population management, understood as the regulating, disciplining and disposing of a person's behaviour undertaken at the level of the body (hence 'bio-power'). But governments soon found that direct and coercive intervention in the lives of its citizens was counter-productive, and in Britain at least this gave rise to policies and practices associated with the notion of liberalism, whereby:

> Responsibilities for various parts of the population and their well-being were moved from a centralized state to ... private or state-funded institutions (schools, hospitals, the military, prisons, charities). At the same time ... practices and technologies of governing in various dispersed sites and institutions ... fed back into centralized state operations in a ... way ... which was both generalized and localized. The logic was generalized in the sense that it helped to cement the processes of regulating individual conduct throughout the social body as a whole. It was localized in that it ... (deployed) a range of techniques and apparatuses (from a parent's monitoring of children's sexual conduct in the home, to the development of physical training procedures in schools) that impacted upon the conduct of each individual – body and soul – within a society. (Danaher et al. 2000: 91–2)

From the perspective of the reason of state the populace was as much a problem as an asset – they were potentially violent, threatening, disruptive, unproductive and a drain on resources. Accordingly the state needed to find ways of ensuring not only that its members were healthy and educated, but also that they were well-behaved and productive. Exercise on its own was not the answer; the set of physical activities collected under the rubrics sport, physical culture and drill had to become what Foucault calls a discursive regime (1997), which can be understood as a "series of rules which determine in a culture the appearance and disappearance of ... events and things" (Foucault 1998: 309). In other words, sport became a way of seeing, experiencing and understanding the world and the self: specifically it worked to produce naturalized dispositions-as-subjects; served as a set of templates against which subjects measured their 'non-coincidence' with themselves; and finally described "the dispersion of subjects", measuring "the interstices" that separated them and the "distances ... between them" (1998: 313). Practices of differentiation between the healthy and the sick, the vigorous and the lazy, and the normal and the deviant were organized through sport-as-discourse: it became, in Foucaldian terms, a 'monument' of Victorian culture (1998: 309). The discourses and practices of sport were particularly useful because they carried out the imperatives of bio-power in an economical way: in sport the body was (at least theoretically) simultaneously exercised, disciplined, educated, disposed and diverted. Elias' notion of sportization fits in with this development quite neatly: it was already a factor in the outlawing, controlling or modifying of blood sports in the eighteenth century (through direct means such as legislation, and indirect ones such as the codification and ritualization of fox hunting), and helped transform the violent melees of folk football into relatively restrained and ordered affairs (thus reducing the instances of injury and death). More importantly it refigured these activities as sites of socio-cultural reproduction (emphasizing the value of team work, competition and self-discipline) and control, so that feelings, passions, disaffections and emotions were dissipated, at a participatory and spectatorial level, within the confined and (more or less) safe spaces of the field and the stadium.

This emphasis on the role of discursive regimes such as the reason of state and sportization is not meant to downplay the significance of the quite dramatic changes to material conditions and contexts that occurred in the nineteenth century (industrialization, urbanization, transport, new communication technologies and Empire): clearly they facilitated the rise of modern sport. But material conditions are always the products of, or at least imbricated with, discursive regimes. As Armand Mattelart and other cultural analysts have demonstrated, an apparently autonomous technological development such as the "internationalization of communications was spawned by two forms of universalism: the Enlightenment and liberalism" (Mattelart 2000: 1). And liberalism itself, along with its various imperatives relating to the free circulation of goods, services, peoples, texts and ideas, arose as a response to and critique of the various interventions (economic, social, political) of government and the reason of state in the lives and affairs of its citizens (Foucault 1997: 75). So if we want to argue that the emergence of modern sport in England in the nineteenth century constituted a (paradigm-shifting) break with the past, then we need to explain how discursive regimes that were produced by, or associated with, the reason of state, the civilizing process, imperialism, nationalism, liberalism and capitalism colonized games (such as cricket and football), to the extent that they helped produce not just the objectivities of the modern field of sport (institutions, specific games, rules, fixture lists, national competitions), but an entirely new set of embodied practices, dispositions and values – what Bourdieu calls the sporting habitus (1991a). In our next section we will define and explain what we mean by the terms cultural field and habitus, and then trace the trajectories of the sporting field within and across various (interconnected) important developments that characterized nineteenth-century British sport.

SPORT AS FIELD AND HABITUS

A cultural field can be said to have come into being when it fulfils at least two criteria. First, it must be able to articulate and manifest itself, simultaneously, as a singularity and a differentiated but cognate group of entities joined together by, and recognizable in terms of, certain core imperatives, values, functions, rules, categories and characteristics. Second, it must be recognized and accepted by, integrated into, and function in compliance with regard to, the network of fields that comprise what Bourdieu calls the field of power (1998). In order for this to happen, a field must have the means and techniques to imagine itself into existence, and then to represent, manifest and valorize itself in a consistent manner to its own members and to other fields. The viability of sport as a cultural field is necessarily predicated, then, on some degree of bureaucratization of people, activities and events within a regime that is specific and universal, changeable and timeless, and above all else iterable. As Allen Guttmann writes:

> Who in actual practice decides the rules of modern sport and who administers the complicated system of research? The answer is obvious. A bureaucratic organization. Once again we need ... to remind ourselves of Max Weber's analysis of the distinction between a primitive hierarchy of prescribed behaviour and a modern bureaucracy of functional roles. We can be sure that the rules of primitive sports changed slowly ... primitive societies are not characterized by bureaucratic organizations of any kind, let alone a sports bureaucracy. (Guttmann 1978: 45)

Institutions, bureaucracies, titles, rules and categories are, however, only the objective manifestation of a cultural field. Fields and their objectivities are simultaneously constituted through and constitutive of a habitus, understood as an ethos and set of dispositions which are embodied by its members, animate and justify its practices, and speak (through and for) the field as a discourse-of-belief. Bourdieu defines the habitus, in *Outline of a Theory of Practice*, as "the durably installed generative principle of regulated improvizations" (1991b: 78). While the habitus is marked by its durability – Appadurai refers to it as a "glacial undertow" (1997: 56) – every cultural field is inflected, to some extent, by both the field of power and those factors and contexts that are felt across the wider social field. This requires improvizations, which taken cumulatively gradually produce different ways of seeing and experiencing the same types of activities. Elias writes that, with regard to hunting, its earlier forms:

> imposed on their followers few restraints. People enjoyed the pleasure of hunting and killing animals in whatever way they could ... Sometimes masses of animals were driven near the hunters so they could enjoy the pleasures of killing without too much exertion. For the higher ranking social cadres, the excitement of hunting and killing animals had always been to some extent the peacetime equivalent of the excitement connected with killing humans in times of war. (1993b: 161)

The influence of the 'civilizing process' transformed the way hunting was understood and played out, a change manifested in both the elaborate ritualizing of fox-hunting and the forms of pleasure it gave rise to:

> A glance back at the earlier forms of hunting shows the peculiarities of English fox-hunting in better perspective. It was a form of hunting in which the hunters imposed on themselves and their hounds a number of highly specific restraints. The whole organization of fox-hunting, the behaviour of the participants, the training of the hounds, was governed by an extremely elaborate code ... Fox-hunting gentlemen killed, as it were, by proxy – by delegating the task of killing to the hounds ... (and) part of the enjoyment of hunting become a visual enjoyment; the pleasure derived from doing it had been transformed into the pleasure of seeing it done. (161–2)

As Elias suggests, one of the "crucial problems confronting society in the course of the civilizing process" was that of finding a "new balance between pleasure and restraint", which led to the "progressive tightening of regulating controls over people's behaviour and the corresponding conscience-formation" involving the "internalization of rules that regulate more elaborately all spheres of life" (1993b: 165). Sport became central to this process, not as a set of disparate activities but as an increasingly pervasive and institutionally valorized (by the fields of government, journalism, religion and education) discursive regime. It is not unreasonable to suggest that by the end of the nineteenth century the status, popularity and institutionalized nature of activities such as cricket, football, rugby and athletics testified to the transformation of a more or less random collection of games and physical activities into a recognizable and relatively autonomous cultural field, with a concomitant set of values, logics and dispositions, animated by and reproduced through a distinctive habitus. This was manifested in various ways, such as the spread and influence of the idea of the superiority of participating in games rather than simply winning them; the production of the body as a critical site of pedagogy and discipline; new forms of pleasure-as-spectatorship; the forging of a sense of communal identity through an association with sporting teams; and perhaps most significantly, the development of an entirely new relationship to the notion of play.

Where and when does the field of sport – and the ideas and discourses that animated it – begin to begin? Consider the following passage from Richard Holt's *Sport and the British* (1989), which refers to the attitudes and practices that characterized late Victorian public schools:

> Whereas boys who loved sports might have been pronounced 'idle' by earlier generations, Victorian schoolmasters were inclined to reserve that word for those who did not care for games. 'Any lower boy in this house who does not play football once a day and twice on half holiday will be fined half a crown and kicked', read a notice at Eton, whose headmaster from 1884 until 1905 was Edmond Warre, a former Fellow of All Souls whose enthusiasm for the classics was only surpassed by his dedication to the Eight. (1989: 76)

Like many other traditions that came into being in the Victorian period, the status of sport and games as being integral to English national character and culture was a fiction that traced its origins back to conveniently idealized times and places: in this case Thomas Arnold's Rugby School and, before that, the agonistic festivals of classical Greece – which partly explains why so many classical scholars (such as Warre) were also sports enthusiasts. In fact, as many sports scholars are at pains to point out (Mangan 1981; Hargreaves 1987; Holt 1989), Thomas Arnold had no interest in games, being completely "insensitive to the possibilities of an athletic ethos with team games as the instrument of moral conditioning" (Mangan 1981: 16); and up until the middle of the century there seems to have been at least as much antipathy towards games as there was support, both at public schools and within the universities (Holt 1989). This changed radically after 1850: the "increased number of boarding-schools helped the development of games", and the "acceptance of organized sport as an important part of school life was now shared by headmasters of old and new establishments alike" (Money 1997: 66).

What were the circumstances that contributed to this transformation? The period from the 1820s to the 1840s saw numbers drop dramatically in most public schools because of their "obvious defects – the barbaric living conditions, the narrow syllabus, the neglect of religion, and the gross indiscipline" (Money 1997: 64). However, the rise of a new, wealthy middle class had "created a widening demand for education, especially boarding education" (Mangan 1981: 15). Arnold was the first to take advantage of this situation, restoring the "soiled and tattered reputation of the public schools" and reassuring the "new middle-class clientele that their sons would be safe in his bosom" (15). So at one level Arnold and the system that followed him took on the task of educating the rising middle class and integrating them into the (previously aristocratic) dominant social fabric. Allied to this was a second, and equally important, contemporary class-based context and utility, predicated on the social unrest manifested in the Charterist movement and the wider "socialistic claims of the oppressed" (Hargreaves 1987: 39): Britain needed leadership from "Christian gentlemen, men who were disciplined, socially responsible and self-reliant enough, not only to govern themselves but the lower orders as well" (39).

How did games-as-sport fit into this scenario, and why did the public schools privilege physical team sports such as rugby, football, cricket and rowing over individual (and to some extent more technical) games and activities such as gymnastics, tennis or golf? In English public schools, team games such as football and rugby served as the means of accommodating and developing the concept of agonistics with regard to less rarefied virtues. Unlike Greek athletics, the Renaissance courtly tradition of formal and technical exercise or German gymnastics, football and cricket clearly weren't vehicles for what were widely considered to be the effete pursuits of physical beauty, the harmonious configuration of body and spirit, or intellectual refinement – and moreover they required no master or overseer. Their primary function was to develop a form of character, broadly understood as an amalgam of self-reliance, loyalty, endurance, teamwork and self-sacrifice.

This experience of team sport supposedly equipped boys with a set of transferable skills and strengths that could be applied to important sociopolitical spheres such as government, business or colonial administration. At one level this was explicable in terms of the fairly conventional notion of the body being trained and learning to endure and overcome physical and psychological stress and pain for the greater benefit of the team. This neatly encapsulated the apparent contradiction that public school sport developed leadership by fostering a culture of self-abnegation: the leader was not so much an individual in the sense of the Hollywood hero who imposes his will on others, but rather an exemplar. In other words, Victorian leaders best embodied and practised the strengths and virtues of (the class factions that stood in for the) the community – and thereby taught and propagated what it meant to be British or English. But at a second level it also provided these leaders-in-waiting with a set of durable beliefs, dispositions, attitudes and a bodily hexis – a habitus – that served as a marker of socio-cultural distinction and reinforced, valorized and justified power differentials at the level of class, race and gender. Boys would leave a public school secure in the belief that, firstly, they were English gentlemen and secondly, that there was a necessary articulation between that identity and moral, physical and cultural superiority – and further down the track, military, social, political and economic success. Immersion in this culture generated a series of performances that were strictly scripted, choreographed and foreclosed: it was an article of belief that the world would follow suit. To take a popular example, Scott of the Antarctic and Captain Oates ('I'm going outside – I may be some time') couldn't be judged on their results so much as their form, which naturally enough was flawless. Like a rugby player who tackles, chases and struggles long after the game has gone, their failure was heroic and especially laudable. This partly accounts for the strong anti-intellectual culture in public schools: determination, action, strength and endurance defined masculinity, while boys were taught that "most material forms of intelligence were slightly effeminate" (Mangan 1981: 106).

Let's consider this relationship between team games, the notion of a sporting ethos and the pedagogical process that produces the relevant habitus, by way of an analysis of the game of cricket as it was played in English public schools of the mid-nineteenth century (and to some extent even today). Theoretically, players were simply taking part in a physical activity defined and delimited by a codified set of rules; but if that's all they were doing, it certainly wasn't cricket. The saying 'it isn't cricket', which passed into the wider socio-cultural field as an indicator of a mode of behaviour that is (ethically or morally) unacceptable, is predicated on an understanding and acceptance of the notion of fair play, which is a very different thing from an adherence to rules. To give some examples, if a player bowls a ball and the person batting gets an edge that isn't detected by the umpire, the correct thing for the batter to do is to 'walk'. Similarly, if an umpire rules incorrectly that a fielder has caught a hit on the full, the fielder should automatically own up to the fact that the catch wasn't taken.

In most cases the fact that someone is playing cricket means they have to be treated as if they are adherents to the ethos of fair play. In other words, it isn't cricket to act as if or suggest that what the opposition is doing isn't cricket: if you believe in the ethos, then you have to believe in its more or less ineluctable efficacy. So if a person batting hits the ball and the umpire is unsure whether the catch has been taken, the correct form is for the batter to ask of the fielder, by as unobtrusive a means as possible (say, a raising of the head as half-posed question), if the ball was caught; for the fielder to nod; and for the batter to immediately and undemonstratively accept this by walking off. What we're dealing with here is not so much a set of practices that accord with playing fairly (you don't cheat), but rather the notion of fair play as pure form. Players were required to demonstrate, in an unobtrusive and natural manner, that winning wasn't the most important consideration – regardless of how important the game was. The extent to which this ethos both produced and foreclosed certain kinds of bodily hexis and practices can be seen in Derek Birley's account (1995), barely believable today, of the scandals that were occasioned by batters firstly going down the wicket to hit the ball on the full or half volley, and secondly playing a pull or hook shot. Moving down the wicket was considered to be not the done thing because it smacked of deliberation and calculation, while the pull and hook were considered ungainly strokes that took excessive advantage of an opponent's lack of ability or loss of control.

The reluctance on the part of cricket players to take advantage of these strategies and techniques demonstrates Bourdieu's point that, with regard to the habitus, the logic of things should never be mistaken for the things of logic (2000); but more importantly it shows the extent to which the public school sports ethos functioned simultaneously as a form of distinction and discipline. Seeming to do everything in an effortless, confident, assured and disinterested manner were markers that distinguished the upper from the lower classes, and naturalized the power differentials that separated them.

When labourers or mechanics played sport, they not only tried too hard – they looked like they were trying. Their ultra competitive, utility-driven behaviour was translated as a cynical disregard for the spirit of the game, and just another manifestation of their selfishness and lack of any kind of a civilizing influence, which by extension valorized the exclusion of their class from decision-making apparatuses. As long as this notion of the value of team work and embodied disinterestedness maintained a doxic status (that is to say, it permeated the socio-cultural as a kind of productive and taken-for-granted truth) it spoke to both the upper and the lower classes, reinforcing the superiority–inferiority binary that defined and determined everything about the way they related to each other. And the message to the middle class was equally clear: public schools, and the team games they played, taught your sons to fit, as seamlessly as possible, into the world of the dominant class.

The propagation of this sporting ethos within public schools was clearly part of a configuration of discourses – albeit a particularly privileged one – that generated and rationalized social, cultural, political and economic practices in Victorian England. Public schools and their games culture were central to the way the civilizing (and more broadly, nationalizing and imperializing) processes was played out, despite the relatively small percentage of the population who had direct experience of it, to the extent that by the end of the Victorian period, sport and the notion of fair play was (almost universally) synonymous with British national character. One of the reasons for this was that the civilizing process was predicated on the value accorded to teamwork, whether at the level of competitive games or politics. We made the point that competition within a game was always subordinated, to some extent, to recognition of and belief in the inviolability of a shared form of behaviour – what Bourdieu calls illusio (1998). When players were matched in a cricket game or politicians disputed over policies or fought out an election, they did more than just work together; they also collectively committed to the system, its values, ideals, discourses and hierarchies as being 'worth the candle'. What follows from illusio is effectively a form of misrecognition which authorizes social groups (based on class, gender, nationality, race, age and education) to, amongst other things, perpetrate and justify acts of symbolic (and physical) violence which seem to contradict their communal ethos. It functions as a form of (convenient and self-serving) forgetting in which violence is transformed into something else; so class domination becomes a form of necessary paternalism, and colonialism the white man's burden.

It is a testimony to the regard with which the ethos of fair play was held – and therefore to the efficacy of the process of misrecognition – that this sense of belief often extended to the most obvious victims of the colonial system. There is a particularly good representation of this in the recent Indian film *Lagan*, where an arrogant English officer agrees to play a game of cricket against a team of local cricketing neophytes, with the stakes being the onerous taxes imposed on the local village. As the game is played out, two things become apparent. First, cricket is shown as being an ideal means for teaching and training the hybrid collection of Indians (Sikhs, Untouchables, Brahmins, Hindus, Muslims) to overcome their differences and to work and believe in themselves as a team/community: cricket is the 'between us' that will eventually imagine the Indian nation into existence. Second, the system works and delivers: the game is won by the locals when one of the English umpires no-balls the English fast bowler on what should have been the last delivery of the game, allowing the hero one more strike, which he despatches for the winning runs. The English captain is enraged and attempts to intimidate the umpire into changing his ruling, to no avail; this is cricket, and the umpire's identification and loyalty is to the game rather than to Britain, the Empire or his race.

FROM PLAY TO SURVEILLANCE

We have discussed how the public school sporting ethos produced this sense of misrecognition, but how was this relation between school pupils and the system maintained? The explanation is that the public schools took the various apparatuses and techniques of surveillance that were employed to monitor and discipline the populace and deployed them "for the first time, on the sons of the dominant classes themselves" (Hargreaves 1987: 42). Hargreaves argues that:

> In the public schools a new disciplinary technology was discovered and developed ... Like the workhouses, asylums, hospitals, prisons, barracks and factories of the era, these schools closed off the individual from society, subjecting him to the uninterrupted gaze of authority. Young adolescent males were 'normalized' by subjecting them to detailed, minute, continuous, comprehensive surveillance in Spartan conditions. Unlike these other institutions, however, what was unique about the public schools was their discovery, development and deployment of the new athleticist technology ... putting it in more conventional terms, the idea that a moral education could be imparted through games, and what they thereby imparted, was their one original contribution to 'educational theory' and practice. Athleticist discourse, the knowledge produced in athleticist practices, and the techniques that were developed, represented an entirely new disciplinary strategy: by extending the gaze of authority beyond work and rest into the world of play, the body was made uninterruptedly visible and control was thereby extended over the 'soul' of the individual (the 'character' in athleticist discourse). (42)

We suggested, in Chapter 2, that play could be defined as a voluntary activity that facilitated an escape from the everyday and its duties, responsibilities and regimes of surveillance. However the "huge games-playing machine" (Mangan 1981: 74) of English public schools was, for many of the public school students who passed through it, neither voluntary nor a form of escape. Richard Holt refers to "A Punch cartoon of 1889" which shows "a headmaster in full academic garb addressing a new boy with the words 'Of course you needn't work, Fitzmilksoppe ... but play you must'" (1989: 97).

Sport became predominantly not just the site where character was learned and developed – it also allowed masters, parents and fellow-pupils to look out for, recognize and take action against forms of behaviour considered deviant or unhealthy. In other words public school sport's version of play-as-education took on the same role as that which Foucault ascribes to the Panopticon – to induce in students "a state of conscious and permanent visibility" (1995: 201).

This invention or colonization of games-as-sport in public schools in Victorian England in the nineteenth century constituted the first stage of the incorporation of sport into the wider disciplinary processes and apparatuses of population management, involving the lower classes, colonized peoples and to some extent women as well. The catalyst for this process, which Hargreaves refers to as 'the expansion of reconstructed sports' (1987), was the desire of ex-public school pupils to spread this distinctive sporting ethos, usually known under the name of athleticism, to the universities and beyond. All the major games played in Britain at this time came under the influence of athleticism, which transformed them into "more differentiated activities, with their own elaborate, codified rules and procedures" (Hargreaves 1987: 45). The most significant feature of this movement – one which allowed for its rapid development into a relatively homogeneous field, embracing and linking games and activities as diverse as professional-ized Association football, amateur rugby, spectator-friendly horseracing and the relatively solitary practice of mountaineering – was precisely its strong organizational and rationalist nature. Sport became the micro-cosmic ver-sion of the macro-cosmic modern state with its remarkably productive and transformative bureaucratic apparatuses, discourses and specialized roles (Guttmann 1978). The scale and complexity of sporting apparatuses and organizations increased, and the discourses and rationales that animated them took on a strong and Eliasian-like 'civilizing tone' as new:

> ruling bodies emerged at the centre to co-ordinate individual sports, adjudicate disputes and formulate policy. New playing techniques were invented and developed and new types of equipment came into use. Roles in sport, both play-ing and administrative, became more specialized. These sports became less like gladiatorial contests and more like scientific exercises in improvement – mat-ters of safer, measured, exact, ordered achievement. Controlling bodies were formed for a number of major sports to co-ordinate the activity of the many sports clubs of different kinds that had sprung up all over the country – the Football Association (FA) in 1863, the Amateur Athletic Club in 1866, the Amateur Swimming Association in 1869 ... Major competitions were inaugu-rated – the FA Cup (1971), the Amateur, Professional and Open Golf Championships (1858–61), the Oxford and Cambridge Boat Race (1849) ... And new major organized sports like tennis, gymnastics, croquet, bicycling and mountain climbing, caught on rapidly. (Hargreaves 1987: 45)

This reconstruction of sport was, as Hargreaves notes, "a major cultural achievement of the mid-Victorian era" (1987: 45). It allowed for individual sports to organize and reproduce themselves, facilitated their incorporation into national and eventually international bodies, and produced many new sites for, and methods of, interpellating individuals, local communities and national groups. But the extent and rapidity of the expansion of sport-as-field – not to mention as a form of popular entertainment and paid employment – was hardly envisaged, or necessarily welcomed, by the ex-public school boys who went on to become colonial administrators, civil servants, lawyers, academics, clergymen, school teachers, bankers and businessmen and who founded, defined and codified most of the significant sports organizations and competitions of the time. For a start there initially was no serious interest in exporting sport to the state school system: drill was considered more relevant to the needs of working-class students, who in any case had no access to playing fields. In fact prior to the 1870s many sports were doing everything they could to limit participation to the 'right types': for instance "the Amateur Athletic Club, founded in 1866 by Oxford and Cambridge men ... was to exclude not only those who had competed in races for money but all manual workers" (Holt 1989: 108); the Amateur Rowing Association did their best to keep out mechanics, "all those who had to work with their hands for a living" (Holt 1989: 108), international crews tainted by professional connections, and even engineers (Birley 1995: 59); and the inclination of educated, middle-class women to take up recreational cycling was considered particularly scandalous.

POPULARIZING SPORT

The question of who was to be allowed to compete in officially sanctioned events and competitions was played out in all major sports, with very different results. Association Football, which had split from rugby in the 1860s over the vexed question of the serious physical injuries arising out of the practice of hacking, was characterized by a form of (unacknowledged) professionalism in the 1860s and 1870s; but the domination of overtly professional northern clubs such as Blackburn Rovers, who won the FA Cup in 1883, threatened to split the sport along professional/amateur and north/south lines. Eventually the Football Association relented and separate professional and amateur football leagues were established in 1885 and 1892 respectively. Rugby union, on the other hand, did split along those lines in 1894, and a new professional code emerged in the form of rugby league, which was a working-class sport played predominantly in Yorkshire and Lancashire (and later in Australia, New Zealand, Papua-New Guinea and France). Although rugby union came to be played world wide, it remained (until recent times) staunchly amateur, at least in theory. In practice, groups such as the Welsh Union were complicit in a culture of what became known as shamateurism: players were rewarded by being given jobs, could claim generous expenses, and periodically found money mysteriously stuffed in their boots or lockers. Scotland, however, "went even further than England to enforce strict amateurism. Scottish rugby began as the preserve of the elite Edinburgh schools ... (and) remained an exclusive game self-consciously distinct from association football" (Holt 1989: 105).

This amateur/professional and north/south divide also characterized cricket, but in an idiosyncratic way. Its history of gambling and entrepreneurial professionalism militated against any adoption of a policy of amateurism as found in rugby, rowing or athletics; but at the same time it was governed, from the late eighteenth century on, by an exclusivist and elitist organization (the Marylebone Cricket Club, or MCC) that was strongly committed to what it saw as the symbiotic virtues of the preservation of the sporting ethos and upper-class governance. As well as presiding, in as conservative a manner as possible, over rules pertaining to bowling actions, the size of the follow-on and other technical matters, it maintained the distinction accorded to supposedly amateur gentlemen by appointing them as MCC team captains, providing them with separate changing rooms, and by publicly distinguishing them from professionals by putting amateurs' initials before the surname and professionals' after. As late as the 1960s:

> the debut of one sixteen-year-old future international was marked, as he proceeded to the wicket, by a loudspeaker announcement apologising for an error on the printed score-cards: 'F. J. Titmus' should read 'Titmus, F. J'. (Birley 2003: 271)

Cricket may have been, as far as the English upper and middle classes were concerned, "the citadel of true sporting values" (Birley 1995: 16), but from the entrepreneurial circuses of the eighteenth century to the time of the professional-in-all-but-name W.G. Grace it was inextricably tied in with, if publicly disdainful of, market forces and money. While it never suffered from "the commercialism and excessive competition that afflicted football" (Birley 1995: 27), it did eventually set up a first-class county league with a fixture list and a points regime – and winners and losers. Moreover the increased success and crowd appeal of the Australian tourists brought an international dimension to the game, which grew to include other members of the British Empire such as New Zealand, South Africa, the West Indies and India. The idea of cricket continued to be caught up in and defined by a public school and village green mythos, and county cricket was never particularly business-like nor lost its upper class affiliations. But the configuration of its status as the national sport and the advent of international competition meant that the MCC was burdened with large if mostly well-behaved and polite crowds, popular press coverage, the star status accorded to its best players, and colonials who were not always white and had never graced the playing fields of Eton.

Football, on the other hand, quickly acquired and embraced a much wider demographic, both in a participatory and spectatorial sense. This process was set in train via the activities of voluntary philanthropic and/or religious organizations concerned about the moral, physiological, and in some cases political health of the lower classes. From the mid-nineteenth century on a variety of organizations, clubs and societies were formed in order to combat the social, political and health problems arising largely out of the massive relocation of populations to industrial urban centres, and the perceived threats that this entailed (in the forms of increased crime, political agitation, and physical and moral degeneration). The lower-class areas of London and the big industrial cities of the Midlands and the North possessed large and growing populations that usually lived in squalid conditions, were often unemployed, and had few socio-cultural facilities, distractions or services at their disposal. Moreover, apart from their working hours, which were closely monitored and regulated, they had little connection with, and were likely to be strongly antithetical towards, the disciplinary mechanisms, discourses and imperatives associated with the reason of state. This was a set of circumstances which, in Foucaldian terms (1995), was produced by power as a challenge to or potential evasion of power, and therefore needed to be met by the more subtle forms of non-state intervention represented by the hygienist movement, temperance leagues, the Boy Scouts, and political, educational or religious groups.

While the strategies and discourses of these philanthropic interest groups weren't uniform (Hargreaves 1987: 59), they frequently made use of sport as one of the prime means of achieving their aims. They filled an obvious need. Although football was played extensively at a kick-about, street level throughout the industrial centres of the Midlands and Northern England, those communities lacked the resources (playing fields, changing rooms, proper equipment, transport, access to communication networks) to transform street games, which were illegal and attracted the interest of police and magistrates, into institutionalized sport. The rapid growth of organized football in these areas, at first on a recreational level and later as a spectator sport, was dependent on church-based groups to the extent that:

> A quarter of Birmingham's teams were church-connected in 1880, and in Liverpool in 1900 local teams originated almost exclusively from church organizations. A significant proportion of the clubs which later formed the core of the Football League were sponsored by socio-religious bodies – among them were Bolton, Wolverhampton Wanderers, Aston Villa, Birmingham City, Swindon, and Tottenham Hotspur. (Hargreaves 1987: 59)

The taking up of sport by state school students was similarly predicated, at least initially, on voluntary activists. Sport wasn't formally introduced into state schools until the last decade of the nineteenth century, to some extent due to a lack of facilities, but also because "there was a belief among influential politicians and educationalists that games were unsuitable for the elementary school child" (Mason 1980: 83). However, the marked increase in the number of school teachers (from 6,395 male teachers in 1870 to 21,223 in 1893 (Mason 1980: 83–4), many of whom had come through the public school system, were "concerned by the physical condition in which some of their pupils came to school" (Mason 1980: 84), and believed strongly in the benefits (physiological, social and moral) of sport, was crucial in overcoming governmental and departmental suspicion-as-inactivity. Although state school students in the 1890s and afterwards continued to drill during school time, after hours they played football and other sports supervised, organized, coached and refereed by volunteers. The result was a network that developed symbiotically and exponentially: teachers organized teams and competitions, products of that system went on to play with professional teams, and those teams and their players sponsored and helped coach and equip more teams, which increased the number of competitions.

As well as church and school teams, football clubs often grew out of, and/or were supported or sponsored by, public houses and businesses. Newton Heath, the precursor of Manchester United, "changed at the Three Crowns in Oldham Road, Manchester, in the 1880s, later removing to the Shears Hotel" (Mason 1980: 27); and this kind of connection (publicans provided pitches, gear and changing rooms, and in return players and fans patronized that pub or hotel) was common in Liverpool, Sheffield, Birmingham, Blackburn and Bolton. Publicans not only helped set up teams, they were "quick to capitalize on the growing interest in football by having the results of matches telegraphed to their establishments where they could be seen free and earlier than elsewhere" (Mason 1980: 27). Arsenal and West Ham, two of the more famous London football clubs, started life in the Woolwich Arsenal and the Thames Ironworks respectively, and the aforementioned Newton Heath "was formed and run, around 1880, by the Dining Room Committee of the Carriage and Wagon Works of the Lancashire and Yorkshire Railway" (Mason 1980: 30).

The spread of organized sport into working- and lower-middle-class urban groups and milieus was a significant stage in the institutionalizing of sport-as-field, but as a process it was not without its tensions and contretemps. As we have seen, the ex-public school groups that were more or less exclusively responsible for defining and bureaucratizing sport were opposed to its popularization, for a number of reasons. First, the whole point of public school sport-as-ethos was that it was elitist rather than populist: it was meant to develop character and leadership in and among male members of the dominant classes, and to function as a form and marker of distinction. Second and concomitantly, it was felt that there was no point in spreading sport and its benefits to groups that, because of their innate inferiority, were incapable of understanding or appreciating them. Third and finally, the efficacy of the relationship between sport and the development of character was predicated on the assumption that upper- and upper-middle-class males could learn or be trained to control and discipline their behaviour in the interest of the team or the group: sport wasn't so much tied up with winning, but with knowing how to lose with dignity and grace while fighting the good fight, doing your best, demonstrating a commitment to teamwork, exemplifying the virtue of self-sacrifice, and above all else maintaining control of oneself. The idea of popular sport, on the other, was disapproved of (by the Football Association, the MCC, the Amateur Athletic Association and other like organizations) because it was associated with winning at all costs; corrupted by professionalism; had developed spectator-friendly competitions that substituted the passivity of watching for participation; and encouraged crowds to be partisan, abusive, disrespectful of authority and violent.

Like any cultural form, however, sport was never going to be limited to the uses that one group had in mind for it. The changing social, cultural, technological and economic contexts in Britain in the second half of the nineteenth century produced conditions that facilitated the development of sport, and football turned out to be the main beneficiary. The shift of increasingly large percentages of the population to cities and urban centres, and the incorporation of men into the workforce as factory workers and clerks, produced two significant imperatives: the desire to make pleasurable use of free time away from the controls and constraints of work, and the need for cultural forms or sites which were linked to, or stood in for, the communities that were being thrown together. While the unemployed men and boys who played kick-about football in the streets were harassed by the authorities, participation in organized teams and competitions was encouraged, as we have seen, by philanthropic groups, school teachers, publicans and industrialists. Moreover those participants were also turning into spectators who felt an identification between themselves and the professional football team:

> Whatever its 'rational' attraction or its suitability in terms of time and space required, the supreme appeal of football lay almost certainly in its expression of a sense of civic pride and identity. The massive expansion in the scale and size of urban communities in the second half of the nineteenth century created new problems of identity for their inhabitants ... In essence, football clubs provided a new focus for collective urban leisure in industrial towns or cities ... As far as playing football or cricket was concerned, the neighbourhood was all important. But the inhabitants of streets ... were members of larger administrative, political, and economic units ... (and they) needed a cultural expression of their urbanism which went beyond the immediate ties of kin and locality. (Holt 1989: 166–7)

Scotland provides the most obvious, complex and ongoing example of this process of interpellation (Althusser 1977) whereby a community is literally 'called into being' via its relationship to and use of particular cultural forms. It occurred at the national level, where the annual game against England reprized Culloden and Bannockburn and every act of colonialist and imperialist violence directed against the Scots, but as Richard Holt points out the significance of the international match:

> grew out of the very disunity of Scottish football itself. The conflict between Celtic and Rangers was no ordinary club rivalry; nor was it confined to Glasgow. Celtic and Rangers drew support from a wide area of central and southern Scotland ... Rangers supporters, bolstered by Orange immigration from Ulster around the turn of the century, saw themselves as bastions of true Scottishness in contrast to the Catholic Irish immigrants, whose numbers were undermining the native Protestant traditions of Scotland and who even wore the colours of a separate national movement. Significantly neither Celtic nor Rangers, despite their wealth, were inclined to buy players from England ... It was only through their joint hostility to England that the two opposing traditions could recognize fleetingly their common loyalty to Scotland. (1989: 257–8)

CONCLUSION

If we look at the uses to which football, and sport in general, were being put to use in middle- and lower-class Britain in the second half of the nineteenth century, and contrast that with its upper-class origins and functions, we can understand why the cultural field of sport evolved into such a schismatic, even schizophrenic, form. Public school-educated elites defined sport, first and foremost, as an ethical activity that was unsuited to people from a lower-class background – not to mention women and non-Anglo-Saxon races and even engineers – while simultaneously equating its exclusivist ethos with the national character. In other words, while sport was discursively universal, at a practical level it functioned as a marker of exclusivity and distinction. Lower- and middle-class groups, on the other hand, reclaimed football and other once popular games for themselves; but as they developed mass appeal they were increasingly drawn into the orbit of powerful or influential fields such as journalism and the media, education, economics and government.

The field of sport has retained, to the present day, a strong discursive commitment to that original sporting ethos, but at the same time it has been transformed by its close if not symbiotic relationship with those aforementioned fields that, most particularly in Britain, Europe and the United States during the *Belle Epoque*, took advantage of the revolution in transport and communications to expand globally. Sport went with them, and the colonization of the world by British sport has lasted much longer than the political and economic edifice that was the British Empire.

5 Global Sport

INTRODUCTION

In the previous chapter we looked at how the field of sport developed in Britain in the nineteenth century: certain games were taken over, transformed and modernized by English public schools, and the incipient field and its activities – as well as its imperatives, discourses, logics and ethos – were exported to or taken up by the wider social field. By the late nineteenth century sport was clearly established in Britain as a separate and relatively autonomous entity. It had the necessary bureaucratic apparatuses, discourses and self-narratives to articulate itself (what it was and meant, what its values and social functions were, what was inside and outside the field) both to its various constituencies and institutions, and to the field of power and other related fields. Once established it became the site of ongoing struggles over its identity: internally, as evidenced by the amateur–professionalism debate; and externally, to the extent that it had to negotiate, and was strongly inflected by, its close relationships with fields such as economics, politics and journalism.

This ongoing, if very gradual, transformation of sport was accentuated as it spread not just to the working class or to various parts of Britain, but also globally. We know that games were played around the world long before modern sport developed in Britain: highly organized, professionalized and bureaucratized Greek athletic festivals and Roman games and circuses were transplanted to parts of Europe and Asia during the Macedonian, Roman and Byzantine periods; and there is considerable evidence of versions of football, boxing and wrestling across Europe, Africa, Asia, the Americas and the Pacific prior to modern times (Mangan 1999a). However, during the late nineteenth and early twentieth centuries the 'sporting turn' began to replace or dominate folk games in countries such as the United States,

Canada, Brazil, Argentina, Australia, New Zealand, South Africa, India and most of Europe.

There were exceptions to the seemingly inexorable march of sport, for instance in Germany where the *Turning* folk gymnastics movement, founded by Friedrich Jahn, established itself as a kind of antithesis to modernity and its manifestations, most notably sport. The *Turners* and public school sports enthusiasts sought to address the same imperatives (providing discipline, training the body to endure and surpass itself, improving the health and strength of citizens): but while the *Turners* were not "immune from the tendency to quantify, to seek records, or to encourage competition" (Guttmann 1978: 88), they disdained the "anti-spirit of noisy championships" (88); opposed the reinvented Olympics; and "condemned boxing and running and ... denounced modern sports as semitic" (88). Adolf Hitler, an ideological heir of *Turnen* German–Aryan nationalism, dissolved the organization in order to help secure the greater prize of hosting the 1936 Olympics, leaving it to find a second life when some of its Alpine activities were incorporated into the Winter Olympic Games.

The demise of the *Turnen* movement and its incorporation into Olympic sport provides a good example of how a cultural field is perpetually in the process of transforming itself. Every field is involved in at least three sets of relations: first with itself, in terms of its need to negotiate between centripetal or homogenizing forces and various inflections and marginalized or peripheral groups; second with everything that it deems and designates to be 'not itself', and which the field has effectively 'othered' (such as chess, ballroom dancing, professional wrestling); and third with powerful fields, most particularly government, business and the media. As sport spread around the world, this set of relations was played out in every country and sport. On the one hand international governance bodies, usually closely aligned with specific interest groups (at the level of nation, gender, race or class), clearly had an interest in maintaining central authority and control over what happened in faraway places (competitions, rules, codes, equipment), a situation made more pressing as improvements in travel facilitated international contests and competitions (the modern Olympics commenced in 1896, the first football World Cup was staged in Uruguay in 1930). At the same time, however, and precisely because of the incipient nature of international sports governance in the first half of the twentieth century, national bodies were sometimes wary or disdainful of the internationalizing of sport (for instance England did not play in the World Cup until 1950, and as late as the 1950s the English FA initially refused to allow their champion team to participate in the European Cup).

However, this ambivalence was countered by, and in contrast to, the interest shown by those other fields with which sport was configured.

A sport–media–business nexus began to develop in the late nineteenth century, most particularly in the United States where baseball leagues had, from the beginning, operated as businesses. Sporting contests were quickly integrated into telegraph and railroad networks; and the Spalding sporting goods business captured and extended the "expanding market for athletic equipment among middle class Americans" to the extent that it was, in Cashmore's words, "to Fordism as ... Nike (is) to post-Fordism" (Cashmore 2000: 384–5). In Britain the relationship between sport, business and the media was more problematical, especially in cricket, tennis, rugby, cycling and athletics where the public school-inspired mistrust of professionalism held sway. On the other hand, countries within the United Kingdom began playing 'internationals' (in soccer and rugby) in the 1870s, and the close political, economic and cultural links that developed between countries that were part of the British Empire (and later the Commonwealth) provided a catalyst for nascent international sporting competitions and tours that predated the modern Olympic Games by over thirty years.

SPORT, COLONIALISM AND EMPIRE

The parochialism of the field at the turn of the century was no more sustainable, in the long run than the attempts of English public school-dominated organizations (MCC, FA, AAA, BU) to quarantine sport from the lower classes, women, commercial interests, journalists and foreigners. Just as the development of modern sport in Britain was tied in with a configuration of historical movements and events, gathered together under rubrics such as "capitalist development, industrialization, urbanization, and the scientific-technological revolution", so to "the global diffusion of modern sports occurred at the same time as 'the constitution of world markets and colonial empires'" (Guttmann 1994: 4). Guttmann rhetorically asks if it was:

> entirely a coincidence that Great Britain, the imperial power that seized the lion's share of the colonial booty, was the foremost country in the development of modern sports ... Johan Galtug notes suggestively that the 'massive export of (modern) sports' from developed to undeveloped areas followed 'old colonial trade and control lines ... into the last little corner of the world.' The cricket grounds in Bombay and Calcutta are as much the relics of British rule as the Red Fort in Delhi. What can be more obvious than to see not coincidence but causation and to conclude, therefore, that modern sports abetted the imperial expansion that carried them to the ends of the earth? (1994: 4–5)

To understand the significance of sport in British colonial culture and practice, two points need to be appreciated. First, the military, political and economic domination that Britain exerted over areas of Africa, Asia, America and the Asia-Pacific was administered by a vast bureaucratic apparatus staffed largely by recruits from the English public school system, many of whom were highly disposed to evangelize sport. Second, by the late nineteenth century sport exercised an almost hegemonic role within the field of British culture: leaving aside the fact that the field of sport actively excluded half the population, at a discursive level sport and British national identity were inseparable. Moreover, and as we saw in our previous chapter, sport had not only come to replace a 'bookish' education as the mechanism through which racial virtues were developed: the sporting field was also the space in which those virtues were honed, tested, maintained and subject to surveillance. The following account from Guttmann provides some indication of the extent to which this attitude had become institutionalized:

> From 1910 to 1948, men recruited for administrative work by the Tropical African Service were selected with an eye to 'character', and character was equated with athletic ability demonstrated by the candidate at a 'public school'. Between 1899 and 1952, Eton, Harrow, Winchester and the other elitist foundations supplied more than 90 percent of all the officers in the Sudan Political Service. The administrative attention paid to sport was extreme. R. D. Furse, a sports fanatic who had studied at Balliol College, Oxford, handed out application forms with a special section for sports. Furse was by no means unusual. 'In the Sudan the provincial governor of Kassala, R. E. H. Baily, who had played cricket for Harrow and Cambridge, used to circulate a leather-bound book among his staff every morning, in which they were expected to indicate against their names the particular form of exercise they would be taking that afternoon'. The men who had won their 'colours' at Oxford and Cambridge were so prominent in the political service that wits referred to the Sudan as 'the Land of Blacks ruled by Blues'. (1994: 64)

While this emphasis on sport was primarily intended to keep the British from 'going native' – that is, becoming effete, lazy and dissolute – it had other functions that led to it being promoted, sometimes selectively, amongst colonized peoples. The dominant narrative of British colonial administration was that military and political intervention in and domination of the affairs of other (non-white) territories was justified on ethical and racial grounds – it was a case of taking up 'the white man's burden' and endeavouring to lift the native up to their own civilized level. Of course as Homi Bhabha has noted, colonialism "often speaks in a tongue that is forked, not false": it desires to produce (and in fact succeeds in producing) colonial subjects who are "almost the same, but not quite" (1994: 85–6). The quintessential example of this position is Kipling's Indian character Gunga Din, whose fetishistic attachment to all things British leads him to give up his own life to help save the Empire from a mutinous uprising: he is honoured at his funeral, becoming in death what he could never be in life – British.

One of the most prominent senior colonial administrators to take up the challenge of using sport in this manner was Lord Harris, who became Governor of Bombay in 1890 (and was later President of MCC): he "believed that cricket was a gift of god" and had to be passed on to "less fortunate folk" in order to "imbue them with Western modes of thought" (Birley 2003: 164). Cricket in India and many other colonial territories in the nineteenth century was originally organized and played in "exclusive clubs that were open only to Europeans"; this, along with "the cost of equipment together with the extensive capital required for the preparation of wickets and ovals" (Guttmann 1994: 32), seemed to militate against its widespread adoption. However, Harris promoted the game amongst the local population, even organizing tournaments in which Indians took the field against British opponents. Indian equivalents of the English Public Schools such as Mayo College also made use of sport as a means of disseminating, in Lord Hardinge's words, "the precious principles of morality, loyalty and culture" (Birch *et al.* 2001: 26).

While Harris and other imperial administrators were attentive to the usefulness of sport in facilitating imperial devotion and even racial harmony in India (very much for political ends), in practice these imperial–racial divisions remained. Harris himself rarely played against Indians, and when he did the cricket ground was:

> Divided into two sections, one for the Europeans and one for the natives, and no native dared to be seen in the European section ... When the luncheon hour arrived, the English team went off to the Gymkhana club-house, and the Parsees went off to their tents and messed alone. (Guha 2002: 73)

These realities of colonialism existed alongside the notion that a touring cricket team "composed of Hindus, Muslims, Parsis and Englishmen" would lead to the "creation of a Cosmopolitan Gymkhana, where the whole army of caste prejudices and racial antipathies might be clean bowled evening after evening" (Guha 2003: 76). In the late nineteenth and early twentieth centuries this theme was taken up by the various Indian Princes who patronized, and often captained, 'mixed' teams. However, racial, religious and caste divisions were dispensed with only so far as they remained within the space reserved for play. Palwankar Baloo, the best Indian bowler of his time and an Untouchable, was eventually invited to play for the Brahmin-dominated Poona Hindus against an English team:

> but at a price. On the field the upper-caste cricketers touched the same ball as he, but off it they observed the ritual taboos. At the tea interval ... Baloo was served the liquid outside the pavilion, and in a disposable clay *matka*, while his colleagues drank in white porcelain cups inside. If he wished to wash his hands

and face, an Untouchable servant of the club took a kettle out into a corner of the field and poured water from it. Baloo also ate his lunch off a separate plate, and on a separate table. (Guha 2003: 90)

Allen Guttmann suggests that while cricket may not have been "intrinsically more susceptible to hierarchical distinctions of social class than other games", it was "associated, more than any other sport, with the British ruling class" (1994: 39). This clearly gave cricket a degree of cultural capital that attracted not just "higher-caste anglophiles" (Guttmann 1994: 39), but other groups who wished to mimic imperial ways such as the Parsis, who "allied themselves with the British to great mutual benefit" in commercial matters, and "Far quicker than the Hindu or the Moslem ... took to Western dress, Western music ... the English language ... (and) cricket, too" (Guha 2003: 12). Precisely because cricket was sanctioned by the colonial regime, it was far more likely to be played widely at an organized level (because grounds were available, or because elite schools considered it a valuable part of a boy's education), which in turn helped to produce local exponents who could make a living from the game and go on to serve as a focus for spectator and media interest. The aristocratic batsmen Ranjitsinhji and Duleepsinhji became household names across the Empire, not just India; and the aforementioned Baloo, who was a net bowler at the exclusive Poona club, owed his inclusion in the Hindu side to a press campaign partly fuelled by his employers.

Once cricket started taking on a significant status within Indian culture, it was appropriated as both a public marker of cultural identity and a means of furthering social and political objectives. The Parsis saw it as contributing to their social, cultural, political and economic advancement. Untouchables took up cricket because it provided them with a space to escape caste-based restrictions and prejudice, if only because the sporting ethos seemed to guarantee some kind of level playing field. Nationalists embraced it because some of their most prominent members were involved in cricket; because of its popular appeal (cricket virtually introduced the notion of mass spectatorship into India); and because games (and victories attained) against British teams fuelled patriotic fervour – one newspaper compared a Hindu victory over a colonial eleven in 1906 to the "recent victory of Asia over Europe, that of Japan against Russia on the battlefield" (Guha 2003: 112). Arjan Appadurai suggests that the triumph of cricket in India had:

something to do with the way sport is managed, patronized and publicized ... something to do with the class background of Indian players and thus with their capacity to mimic Victorian elite values ... something to do with the dialectic between team spirit and national sentiment ... which is inherent in the sport and is implicitly corrosive of the bonds of empire

... something to do with the way in which reservoirs of talent is created and nurtured outside the urban elites, so that sport (became) self-sustaining ... something to do with the ways in which media and language (helped) to unyoke cricket from its Englishness ... and it has something to do with the construction of a postcolonial male spectatorship that can charge cricket with the power of bodily competition and virile nationalism. (Appadurai 1997: 91–2)

India's experience of and relation to sport – a complex configuration of historical, cultural, religious, racial, political and economic factors – can't be put forward as an exemplification of the British colonial experience. It is nevertheless a useful case study for identifying some of its motifs, among which we could include the role of ex-public school and university expatriates in popularizing and organizing sports, and helping to establish or inflect a particular sporting ethos; the imbrication of sport and communal or group identity/subjectivities; the tendency of minority and disempowered or disadvantaged groups to make use of sport as a means of attaining social and economic upward mobility; and the rapid incorporation of sports into business and media networks.

It goes without saying that the establishment of sport in the British colonies of Australia, New Zealand, South Africa and in the Caribbean – as with India and the rest of the Empire – was almost exclusively down to the work of ex-public school and university sports enthusiasts. As members of the ruling elites, as administrators, members of the military hierarchy or as teachers in colonial versions of the still exclusive public school system, they had considerable cultural capital, access to financial and other resources, important socio-political and business connections, and the organizational experience and skills requisite for the task. Moreover, as the exemplars of British civilization they were expected to take the lead in transplanting its cultural institutions – and their concomitant virtues and pleasures.

Both football and rugby were introduced into New Zealand between 1860 and 1870 by "public school émigrés" (Baker 1982: 133), and this was also largely the case in South Africa, Canada, Kenya, Sierra Leone, Uganda and the Sudan. In Australia cricket was introduced by the military in the early nineteenth century, and a variety of sports (including rugby union, rugby league, soccer, horseracing, tennis, rowing, athletics and cycling) followed soon afterwards, replicating established British or English institutions, rules and codes of conduct. Even a code as popular and egalitarian as Australian rules football originated in the English-inflected and socially elite Melbourne Cricket Club, and was initially played in "those schools in Melbourne and Geelong to which the sons of the local bourgeoisie were sent". It eventually moved into the suburbs "to be taken up and eventually taken over by the broader community in which the working classes predominated numerically, if not in terms of effective control of the game and its organization" (Hay 2003: 18–19).

The Caribbean, however, provides perhaps the best example of a neat and tidy transplantation of British sporting culture to the colonies:

> The British, who never constituted more than a small fraction of the islands' population, brought the game to the Caribbean for their own amusement. Among the first clubs were St. Ann's on the island of Barbados (1806) and the Trinidad Cricket Club (before 1842). On Barbados, commonly referred to as 'Little England', three 'public schools' attended to the education of the white and black elites: Harrington College, The Lodge, and Cobmermere. The masters, no different from those in other outposts of the Empire, emphasized team sports in general and cricket in particular ... Schoolmasters like Edward B. Knapp were so successful in propagating the 'games ethic' that, when the black lower classes took up the game in the twentieth century, 'the codes and standards to which they aspired were those established and maintained by the culturally dominant cricketing products of the elite schools'. (Guttmann 1994: 28)

This domination had a particular racial – and racist – inflection: even though white cricketers were soon surpassed in number and ability by blacks, control of the West Indian Cricket Board, and captaincy of the test team, remained in the hands of 'white gentlemen' until after the Second World War. Consequently in the period after 1960, when white control had all but passed from West Indian cricket, cricket matches involving England or the MCC and the West Indies often became occasions where sport stood in for a great deal more – such as the redressing of several hundred years of colonial violence. This explains why a white South African expatriate drafted in to play cricket for and captain England, as Tony Greig was in the 1970s, could make a public statement to the effect that the English team hoped to make the touring West Indians 'grovel' by the end of the series; and why at the end of the series the same South African, doubtlessly like many of the other English players who were on the receiving end of the fast bowling of Andy Roberts and Michael Holding "confessed himself frightened for the first time in his life" (Birley 2003: 316). After the tour of Australia in 1960-61, when the collection of disparate countries that came together only as a sporting identity were feted by "a million inhabitants of Melbourne", the Trinidadian cricketer C.L.R. James suggested in his autobiography that "Clearing their way with bat and ball, West Indians at that moment had made a public entry into the comity of nations" (1963: 252).

This connection between sport and national or communal identity seems to have been particularly pronounced in nascent colonial cultures: apart from the transference of the hegemonic role of sport in Britain during the late nineteenth century, there were probably four other main reasons why this was the case. The first of these was that sport, as a cultural field and set of practices, was characterized by a very definite and prescribed ethos, bodily hexis, chain of command, discourses and set of dispositions, rules and codes. Identities, roles, actions, forms of capital and modes of behaviour were relatively unambiguous, which must have held a considerable attraction for communities removed from the certainties and familiarities of home. Second and relatedly, sport had a masculinist inflection, which suited the gender politics of nineteenth-century colonialism. Third, while sporting governance tended to reinscribe British socio-cultural hierarchies, the Indian and West Indian experiences of sport as an alternative space where lower class or dominated groups could compete against their supposed betters on even terms also struck a cord in the more egalitarian cultures of Australia and New Zealand. Fourth and finally, the victories of Hindu or the West Indian cricket team over their English opponents, the Australian victory over the MCC in the first 'Ashes' series of 1882, and the triumphant New Zealand All Blacks rugby tour of Britain in 1905 all came to be seen as the manifestation of a 'communal arrival' on a wider stage. Moreover, sporting contests provided colonial societies with a stage and an occasion for performing group and national identity: sport meant popular spectacles, instant heroes and occasions of theatrical drama and passion – something that was quickly appreciated, exploited and promoted by politicians, entrepreneurs and journalists.

In countries outside the Empire, where British influence was less institutionalized and more transient, sport still made considerable gains – but in a less homogeneous manner. In Europe organized sport was introduced from the 1870s onward, sometimes through British-style public schools (as was the case in Switzerland), but more usually through the work of "visiting or resident Englishmen, who largely made up the early organized teams and at first headed the administrative national associations" (Baker 1982: 134–5). Rugby was played in only a few areas of France, and cricket failed to gain any kind of permanent foothold outside the Empire; but football, which was a "much simpler and inexpensive" and much less elitist game, took Europe "by storm during the last two decades of the nineteenth century" (Baker 1982: 134), and professional leagues were established in France, Germany, Italy and the Austro-Hungarian Empire. Much the same occurred in South America, where British émigrés, businessmen, employers of railroad construction companies and sailors helped set up associations and leagues in Argentina, Brazil, Uruguay and Chile. One of the most famous Brazilian clubs was named after Corinthians, the elite English amateur football team of the 1880s and 90s, and the English club Liverpool still has a namesake in Uruguay.

In most of Asia, as well as the remainder of the America continent, the dissemination of sport and sporting culture was predominantly the result of

American, rather than British, initiatives. During the first decade of the twentieth century missionaries introduced basketball into China, Japan and the Philippines, and baseball was popular enough to support professional leagues in Cuba, Mexico, the Dominican Republic and in various other countries subjected to American cultural and economic influence and/or military occupation. To some extent Canada ended up going the way of Central America, despite its background of close political, cultural, economic and social ties with Britain. In the early nineteenth century British troops joined the city's "ethnically British upper class to form the Montreal Cricket Club", and in Toronto and other "culturally British cities" elite public schools "made sure that the boys were ... taught to play what, as British subjects, we regard as our national game" (Guttmann 1994: 21). But cricket, soccer and rugby never managed to gain the support accorded to the traditional indigenous game of lacrosse or the ice skating version of hockey, favoured by the French-speaking part of the population, which "became firmly established in the second half of the nineteenth century as Canada's premier winter sport" (Baker 1982: 160). As Canada became drawn into the American cultural orbit, basketball, baseball and American football leagues were established and enjoyed wide spectator appeal, without ever attaining the prestige or relationship to communal and national identity that characterized ice hockey.

SPORT IN THE UNITED STATES

Although Canada in a sense simply outgrew its British sports heritage and connections, the United States of America, while borrowing from and being influenced by aspects of the British experience, developed its own version of modern sport. Like Britain, but perhaps to an even greater extent, games and outdoor activities in the seventeenth and eighteenth centuries were subject to the often hostile gaze of Puritan magistrates; and there is relatively general agreement amongst cultural historians and critics that Puritans "hindered the development of modern sports" (Guttmann 1995: 3) because of their suspicion of play and any outdoor activities that lacked utility (that is, promoting health, fitness or useful skills such as fishing or hunting). Moreover, anti-British sentiments ensured that to some extent "the new nation went without the trappings of a sporting society. Sport seemed a waste of time and out of place in a land of hardworking farmers who had but recently renounced a self-indulgent king and hereditary nobility" (Vincent 1994: 16).

At the same time the picture of American games and pastimes in the eighteenth and early nineteenth centuries was still recognizably British.

Southern gentry "were building English-style circular tracks; importing thoroughbred horses; retaining breeders, trainers, jockeys ... and generally making racing a symbol of upper-class life"; and not unlike their English counterparts "impulsively betting entire fortunes on a single race" (Gorn 1997: 38). In the larger and more urbanized northern cities such as Boston, New York and Philadelphia locals formed fishing, hunting and horseracing clubs, and engaged in decidedly non-utilitarian activities such as "balls, plays, dances, horse races, and cockfights" (Gorn 1997: 42). Lower-class activities included the usual pre-modern British fare of wrestling and other forms of physical combat, cockfighting, foot races and fishing as well as lacrosse. What separates America from Britain, at this point, is that the rise of an American equivalent of British consumer society in the late nineteenth century, while producing an attendant increase in the consumption of luxury goods, broadening cultural practices, and the opening up a market for recreational items and equipment (Struna 1997: 17), did not pave the way for the transition to a bureaucratized and professionalized mass spectator sports culture, as was the case in Britain. In Antebellum America "sporting events at their most organized might attract a few thousand spectators", while "The most likely form of 'sport'" were "Folk games and recreations" that "were part of communal preindustrial life ... (and which) grew out of face-to-face relationships, and expressed the tensions and cohesiveness of particular localities" (Gorn 1997: 42).

The United States did, by the end of the nineteenth century, have a sports culture that was socially pervasive and recognizably modern; but there were significant variations, as well as similarities, with regard to what happened in sport in Britain and America. America, like Britain, underwent a process of rapid industrialization and urbanization that gave rise to massive increases in crime, hooliganism, alcoholism, gambling, whoring, ill health, social anomie and excessive sedentary work. Proponents of muscular Christianity and civic reformers (including President Teddy Roosevelt) promoted sport and physical exercise as both an antidote to these vices, and a means of developing the virtues of "courage, hardihood, endurance and self-control" (Riess 1997b: 186). Unlike Britain, America lacked a large, affluent and influential private school system bent on promoting the benefits of sport; but there was the ideological influence of *Tom Brown's Schooldays*, which "had an enormous impact on American educators, intellectuals, and average people, resulting ... in a sporting boom at universities like Harvard in the late 1850s" (Riess 1997b: 179).

To some extent elite universities such as Yale and Harvard played the part of the public schools: they were the sites where games were organized, codified and practised within the wider context of a deliberate sporting ethos. Moreover, American college sport was both elitist and predicated on fulfilling class-based imperatives: the upper-middle-class young men who attended college and played American football (a game similar to the variant of folk football played at Rugby and Winchester) were simultaneously constituting themselves as part of an influential social network and acquiring the leadership skills that would be required of their class and/or that network membership. College football was to this group what rugby was to public school Englishmen, being:

> the kind of game appropriate for a nation ripe for a clean, violent, virile, yet gentlemanly sport. Coming after the carnage of the Civil War in an era dominated by the social Darwinian concept of the survival of the fittest, football ... was, in William James' words, a 'moral equivalent of war' that would teach athletes to be 'contemptuous of softness, surrendering of private interest, and (obedient) to command'. (Riess 1997b: 187)

This class-and-sport network copied its English counterpart in establishing exclusive and supposedly rigorously amateur clubs and governing organizations in athletics, swimming, tennis, baseball, football and rowing. Most of these sports had affiliations with, or directly presided over, what was to become an extremely lucrative system of intercollegiate competitions that developed alongside, and largely corresponded to, the railroad networks that spread across the eastern and central United States after the Civil War. College sport was originally dominated by baseball (the first intercollegiate league was established in 1879) and athletics (1875), but by the 1880s American football games between teams from Yale, Harvard, Princeton and other Ivy League institutions were attracting crowds of forty thousand spectators, and earning athletic associations tens of thousands of dollars in gate money. This surge in spectator numbers and revenue was accompanied by an increase in the competitiveness of sporting competitions; negotiations about and agreement on the standardizations of codes, rules and equipment; a concomitant move towards varying levels of (sometimes unrecognized) professionalism; and the kind of displacement of education by sport that characterized English universities in the late Victorian period, to the extent that the football coach "became one of the most visible people, if not the most important, on campus" and the most successful "were paid more than top professors" (Riess 1995: 125).

Well before college football was codified and institutionalized in the 1870s, America's other main sport, baseball, was in the process of transforming itself from a derided version of cricket into an incarnation of American cultural identity. The beginning of organized baseball is usually traced to the New York Knickerbockers club and its members, a group of middle-class doctors, lawyers and clerks who from 1845 until 1860 occupied the same position with regard to baseball as the MCC in cricket.

They established and presided over changes to the "basic patterns and rules" of the game and promoted a tone and spirit that emphasized "congeniality on the field" (Adelman 1997: 60) rather than competitiveness. As was the case with cricket and soccer in England, however, this Corinthian-like culture went into decline as the spectator appeal of the game increased: a post-Civil War boom led to the formation of numerous professional leagues, including for a brief time a player-run competition. Reflecting the strong business ethos of these enterprises, changes to the rules of play tended to develop as a consequence of commercial interests and demands – as a means of producing more or less hits, or making games more competitive.

While baseball was reduced to or at least integrated into the logics and imperatives of the commercial market, it was also simultaneously removed from and set above that market through its close association with a mythical/pastoral American world manifested in the "sounds of summer, the tap of bat against ball, the cries of the infielders, the wooden plump of the ball into the catcher's mitts" (Guttmann 1994: 51–2). Because of its perceived special place in and relation to American culture, baseball remained inalienable, in a legal sense: in a Federal League case of 1922 "the court decided that baseball was an exhibition and not a business in the sense of the Sherman Antitrust Act of 1890" (Guttmann 1978: 97); and this position was reiterated in rulings in 1957 and again in 1972 (with one Justice indulging in a "lengthy rollcall of the heroes of baseball and his evocation of the glories of the game" (Guttmann 1978: 97), despite the Supreme Court consistently denying the same status to boxing and professional football.

This development, whereby baseball more or less came to 'stand in' for America, was the product of a configuration of socio-political, technological and commercial factors. At one level it was part of a wider rejection of and a distancing oneself from Britain and its class structures, of which baseball's close relative cricket was the exemplar. But there were other "contributing factors, such as greater urban concentration enhancing the prospects for spectator sports, and better rail travel facilitating intercity competition" (Vincent 1994: 93). The Civil War and the subsequent mass movement of populations to urban and industrial centres "traumatically dislocated millions of Americans" (Vincent 1994: 94), and as with their English counterparts in Birmingham, Manchester and Liverpool they found a sense of communal identity and belonging through their involvement in, attendance at, and support of local sporting teams.

Probably the most significant cause of the transformation of baseball from sport into myth, however, was the close relationship that grew up, in late nineteenth century, between baseball (and sport in general) and the fields of journalism/media, entertainment and business – a development predicated

on the rapid establishment and accessibility of mass communication technologies and networks:

> The nearly universal availability of the telegraph was made more effective
> in the 1880s by the adoption of techniques to send several messages
> simultaneously over the same wire. Pool rooms and saloons all over America
> installed receiving sets to keep their customers up-to-date regarding nationally
> important baseball scores ... The establishment of mass journalism is explain-
> able by the waiting for words by the literate population and the exploitation of
> techniques for high-speed typesetting and printing. Much of the news came
> from wire services and the news that increased circulation most was sports
> news. (Mandell 1984: 184–5)

Prior to the Civil War, and as was the case in Britain, sports news had
appeared intermittently in American newspapers and journals, often as an
adjunct to social news; but by the 1890s there were separate sports pages.
The popularity of sport, and baseball in particular, was given an enormous
boost by increased newspaper coverage that often worked in tandem with
highly successful public relations campaigns run by sports entrepreneurs
such as Albert Spalding. Partly as a consequence of the horizontal integration he developed across his manufacturing and marketing operations,
Spalding was a pivotal figure in popularizing sports participation worldwide: he mass produced, promoted and standardized tennis equipment;
helped to initiate the bicycle fad at the turn of the century by developing
faster, safer and cheaper machines; and represented American sports at the
Paris Universal Exposition of 1905. His focus, however, was on baseball: he
started out as a player and later became a manager and team owner, a
chronicler and historian of the game, a tour promoter and the official sup-
plier of bats and balls to the professional leagues. He also literally brought
about a rewriting of baseball history so as to more firmly establish a corre-
spondence between it and American cultural heritage and identity. The
game's pastoral associations and national integrity were inscribed and naturalized by way of the invention of a myth of:

> Abner Doubleday and his Cooperstown cow pasture ... in order to wipe away
> the memory of the game's actual invention, in its modern form, by a New York
> bank clerk named Alexander Cartwright. The myth of Abner Doubleday was
> cut from whole cloth in 1907, when Spalding appointed a commission, chaired
> by his friend Abraham Mills, to investigate the origins of baseball. The rigged
> nationalistic commission which put the undeserving Doubleday in the ludic
> pantheon was determined to disprove the (correct) theory that baseball was
> derived from the British children's game of rounders. On the basis of a
> letter from an octagenarian named Abner Graves, Mills obligingly informed
> the delighted Spalding that the game was an American invention. (Guttmann
> 1994: 52)

THE MODERN OLYMPIC GAMES

The situation with turn-of-the-century baseball in a sense epitomized the field of sport as it was developing in the United States – away from, and in contradistinction to, what was happening in Britain and the British Empire, and to some extent the rest of the world. There were a number of continuities and shared characteristics that continued to mark sport, regardless of where it was located, as a still relatively homogeneous field, such as the pervasive and highly influential place of athletics and other forms of exercise within the fields of health and education; the strong identification between communities and local and national sporting teams; the maintenance of a strong discursive commitment to an ethos of fair play and the benefits of agonistics; the development of regular national and international competitions and tournaments; and the internationalizing and/or global networking of governance organizations. At the same time the early twentieth century American experience of a strong connection between sport with the fields of business and journalism/media was not universally replicated for perhaps another seventy years or so. This was demonstrated in the difference, for instance, between the enthusiastic acceptance of the sporting broadcasts of boxing, baseball and college football games in the United States, as opposed to the suspicion of and resistance to live coverage of cricket and association football in England (Boyle and Haynes 2000).

The tensions that arose within the field of sport over issues such as amateurism versus professionalism, the relation between sport and national politics, and the role of the media and business in representing and marketing sport are tied up with the distinction we made earlier between cultural activities that are, in Bourdieu's terms, either autonomous or heteronomous (1995). The relative autonomy of a field, which can be defined in terms of and measured with regard to "its ability to reject external determinants and obey only the specific logic of the field, governed by specific forms of symbolic capital" (Johnson 1993: 15), is often an index, one way or another, of its cultural significance and status. The legal field is, in most places and contexts, powerful enough to enjoy a certain degree of autonomy, and to institutionalize and naturalize that by way of legislation. Aztec anthropology or Classics, on the other hand, maintain their autonomy precisely because they are generally regarded as having little or no relevance to the wider social field, and therefore they escape the gaze of and interference from the field of power. Of course every field is connected, in some way, with the wider social, but the manner and extent to which that connection is manifested (and impinges upon its autonomy) varies because each field is:

a social universe with its own laws of functioning. External determinants can have an effect only through transformations in the structure of the field itself.

In other words the field's structure refracts, much like a prism, external determinants in terms of its own logic, and it is only through such refraction that external factors can have an effect on the field. The degree of autonomy of a particular field is measured precisely by its ability to refract external demands into its own logics. (Johnson 1993: 14)

The manner which the field of sport refracted external determinants during the period from the late nineteenth to the middle of the twentieth century can best be exemplified through reference to the history of the modern Olympic movement. We pointed out previously that Baron Pierre de Coubertin, the founder of the modern Olympic Games, had been strongly influenced by the sporting ethos that developed in English public schools, as well as the idealized account of sport that appeared in Hughes' 1864 novel *Tom Brown's Schooldays*; and in one sense the inflection he gave the first games (held in 1896) represented a world – and more specifically a field – which was in the past, or at least in the process of passing away. Initially Coubertin's ideas about the utility of sport were informed by notions of patriotism and jingoism: sports, training and exercise would produce fitter and more disciplined Frenchmen who could match the *Turnen*-trained Prussians, victorious in the war of 1870. But by the early 1890s when he was working seriously towards reviving the Olympics, Coubertin:

had begun to outgrow the vindictiveness that had originally motivated his interest in sports. Modern technology – steamships, railroads, the telegraph and the telephone – had begun to transform the world into a 'global village', and ... Coubertin ... was increasingly drawn into the humanistic vision of a peaceful world. Sports were still the means, but the ends had been transformed. (Guttmann 1992: 10–11)

There had been several English revivals of the ancient Olympics from the seventeenth century onward, and the Greeks staged games as part of a culture of nationalistic revival, on and off, throughout the nineteenth century. A number of factors militated against the continuity or institutionalizing of these attempts, however, including the absence of the kind of organizational and administrative apparatuses that eventually characterized the newly emerging field of sport; and their disconnection from wider social, political, economic and technological networks and forces. To some extent the field of sport, despite having spread across and firmly established itself within the British Empire, Europe and North America, remained insular, chauvinistic and relatively out of touch with what Mandell refers to as "the advancing freedom of movement of so many Europeans and the idealistic cosmopolitanism of the time" (Mandell 1984: 200). What Coubertin and his supporters effected, with regard to sport, was both to bring about its inclusion in "the great cultural manifestations of the late nineteenth century" (Mandell 1984: 199), of which the World Fairs were the most obvious example, and to accelerate its integration into the processes, logics and networks of international governance, co-operation and standardization:

> The Paris Universal Exposition of 1878 was the first to include international congresses for such diverse specialists as dentists, historians and statisticians. This ... led to further internationalism of all sorts in the nineteenth century. The universal postal union had already been established in 1875. There was a convention to standardize patent laws in 1893 and one to standardize copyright in 1887. The Paris exhibition of 1889, for which the Eiffel Tower was built, included a vast range of instructional exhibits and international meetings of scholars, scientists, and academic specialists. (Mandell 1984: 199)

The first of the modern Olympics, held in Athens in 1896, was an unlikely amalgam of the 'interested disinterestedness' (Bourdieu 1991a) of English public school sport, and the more overtly parochial approach of the host nation and American athletes. American supporters, rather than evincing gentlemanly polite appreciation, "hissed and shouted and behaved like overgrown children" (Guttmann 1992: 18), while the blatant nationalism, self-aggrandisement and opportunism of the Greek organizers was dressed up in Coubertin's internationalist rhetoric of "harmony and good will in sports and to universal peace" (Guttmann 1992: 20). The next two games – in Paris and St Louis – were subsumed within world fairs, and attracted mostly local participants and spectators – and scant media attention; but by the time of the 1908 London games things were beginning to change. For a start England, as the home of modern sport, was well equipped to provide the infrastructure, organizational prowess and experience, and the spectator and media interest that previous games had lacked. Moreover there was increased international interest, with a concomitant rise in the level and intensity of competition. Success or failure at the Olympics became connected with national status, pride and politics, both in Britain and elsewhere. As a consequence disinterestedness, harmony, good will and universal peace quickly went out the window:

> As sports contests, the games of the Fourth Olympiad were quite successful, but they were marred by unusually strident nationalism ... The most controversial political question of the day was the fate of Ireland (where) ... the mostly Roman Catholic Irish were still ruled by the mostly Protestant British ... Irish American athletes were many ... As the teams marched into the stadium on opening day, national flags fluttered, but the Stars and Stripes hung at half-mast ... Many British spectators were convinced that this ... was a slap in the face for the king and queen ... When competition began, the officials, all of whom were British, were accused of bias ... the British press denounced the Americans for their lack of good sportsmanship ... *The Times* (London) (concluded) that the perfect harmony which everyone wished for had been marred by certain

regrettable disputes and protests, but the editors took comfort in the illusion that athletes and officials departed London with their friendship unimpaired. (Guttmann 1992: 29–30)

Previous games had seen disputes over political issues (Athens, for instance, had to deal with and resolve the 'sporting status' of countries within the Austro-Hungarian empire), but the playing out of the opposition to the British occupation of Ireland on the athletics track, and the pointed fact that President Theodore Roosevelt greeted the United States team on their return, were signs that organized sport, and the Olympics in particular, had irrevocably drifted into the field of international relations. Nations intent on increasing their international profile quickly recognized this: Japan, fresh from their 'coming out' military victory over the Russians, joined the IOC in 1912; Sweden "employed the festival to demonstrate to their visitors and to the world's newspaper reading public their prominence on the world scene" (Mandell 1984: 209); and the would-be games of 1916, interrupted by the First World War, were considered to be of such significance to Imperial German prestige (and in keeping with the Kaiser's "well-known delight in sport spectacle" (Mandell 1984: 210) that an American track star was employed to coach German track athletes and help them to become internationally competitive (Mandell 1984: 210).

Los Angeles in 1932 was, for Coubertin, little more than "propaganda for tourism" (Kruger 2004), but the staging of the 11th Olympiad in Berlin was more to his liking. Cashmore writes that "Rarely has a sporting event been used so blatantly for propagandist purposes" (2000: 201), although Coubertin thought that it had "magnificently served the Olympic ideal" (quoted in Guttmann 1992: 70). Hitler was quite a late convert to the games and to sport in general: he had an affiliation with the *Turnen* movement, and their unabashed nationalism and race-consciousness was closer to his ideals than the rhetorical humanism of modern sport, which had been condemned by a Nazi spokesperson in 1932 as being "infested with Frenchmen, Belgians, Pollacks and Jew-Niggers" (Guttmann 1992: 54). Unlike *Turnen* festivals, however, the Olympic Games were prestigious global events that offered an unparalleled opportunity "to demonstrate German vitality and organizational expertise" (Guttmann 1992: 55).

The Marxist theorist Jean-Marie Brohm's contention that the Olympics had been "proto-fascist from the beginning, and ... could be staged to perfection only in a fascist country" (quoted in Kruger 2004: 48), was not altogether wide of the mark. The overtly racist and pro-Aryan tone of the Munich games simply reprised what was, more or less from the beginning, a salient characteristic of the Olympic movement, and of modern organized (Western) sport in general. Institutionalized racism in Britain and its empire and in the United States, for instance, was consistently refracted in terms of the logics, discourses and practices of the field of sport. The attempted international boycott of the Berlin Olympics partly failed because the American Olympic official and future IOC President Avery Brundage was convinced that it was "a conspiracy of Jews or Communists" (Guttmann 1992: 60), neither of whom were held in particularly high esteem by Brundage and the rest of the predominantly white, upper-class male members of the IOC.

American sensitivities about the racism of the Berlin games did not extend to their own local policies and practices, which in a sense were as openly and systematically racist as any sports culture in the world, including that of Nazi Germany. At the beginning of the twentieth century, Afro-Americans were largely forced out of mainstream cycling, horseracing, hunting, baseball, football, tennis and swimming; inter-racial boxing bouts were often prohibited by law, and the dominance of heavyweight black fighters such as Peter Jackson, Jack Johnson and Sam Langford "set off a frantic search" (Guttmann 1994: 123) for a 'great white hope' of American boxing who would put Negroes in their place. Moreover it was dangerous for Negroes to use public beaches or openly celebrate the victory of a black boxer such as Johnson. They were also deprived of public parks and spaces: the "first black municipal park in Birmingham, Alabama, opened in 1908, only after seventeen white parks were constructed" (Riess 1995: 107).

This decidedly political inflection to early twentieth-century sport extended to the area of gender. Allen Guttmann is correct in warning that "Blanket statements about the pre-nineteenth century exclusion of women from sport are commonly uttered in blissful ignorance of the historical record" (1991: 1); but women's involvement in organized sport in England in the nineteenth century was clearly limited by a strongly held perception, often supported by what passed as scientific research, that their participation in most forms of physical exercise was harmful to their health and child-bearing capacity, not to mention degrading to their femininity. Both Coubertin and the IOC (and its all-male members) were generally opposed to the participation of women in sport: as well as the usual moral and health-related objections, Coubertin "disapproved of women's involvement in public competitions" because the male spectators "who gathered for such competitions didn't show up to look at sports" (Guttmann 1991: 163). James Sullivan, the American organizer of the St Louis Olympics, ensured that "archery was the only sport in which women were allowed to compete" (Guttmann 1991: 163). A significant battle did erupt regarding the inclusion of women's athletics in the 1932 games, after a *New York Times* article complained about the unfortunate sight of exhausted and breathless women at the completion of the 800 metre race in Amsterdam in 1928 (Guttmann 1991). Notwithstanding their concern, shared by various American sporting and physical education organizations, women were eventually allowed to run, jump and throw, as well as swim, skate and fence at the Los Angeles Olympics in 1932.

The case of the *New York Times* article alerts us to one more significant development in the field of global sport – the increased role played by the media in representing, analyzing, promoting and influencing major sporting activities. The Americans had been the first to include sports pages in daily newspapers in the 1890s (Boyle and Haynes 2000), and Britain and the European continent soon followed suit. By 1900 dailies such as the *Express*, *Mirror* and *Daily Mail* were heavily involved in reporting and sponsoring soccer, cricket and golf, and the popularity of Ashes contests between Australia and England boosted the international coverage of test matches by newspapers and eventually BBC radio. In Europe at the turn of the century specialist sports newspapers such as *L'Equipe* (in France) and *Gazzetta dello Sport* (in Italy) were launched to cater for the public's demand for news of football, motorsports and cycling. Like the British dailies they were drawn, by commercial logics, into a kind of symbiotic relation with the field: *L'Equipe's* founder Henri Desgrange, for instance, invented the idea of the Tour de France cycling race as a means of increasing his paper's circulation. Media coverage of the earliest Olympics had been sporadic, but this changed with the Los Angeles and Berlin games. In Los Angeles the film community helped promote the games, ensuring wide media interest, and the organizers had boosted their profile by disseminating a newsletter to the world media. Goebbels and Hitler had already demonstrated their appreciation and mastery of the power of communication technology and media-as-spectacle: during the German elections of 1932 the Nazis had made use of phonograph records, illustrated magazines and propaganda films along with the usual banners and posters (Fest 1977: 473). The extent and co-ordination of media activities used to promote the Berlin games, however, made this pale into insignificance:

> By October 1934 the propaganda committee was providing 24,000 copies of its newsletter worldwide ... This included 3,075 foreign newspapers and jour-nals ... the travel offices of the Germany railway abroad started to advertise the Olympic Games as the best place for a holiday ... the press service was enlarged and ... translated and printed in fourteen languages ... Olympic placards were distributed complete with logo in nineteen languages and a total press run of 156,000 copies ... leaflets were distributed in fourteen languages and a press run of 2.4 million. The ten days of the torch run from Olympia to Berlin received the full attention of every aspect of the German media. As well as spreading the good word, the committee countered the bad. Press conferences stressed the peace message of the games in which the host nation fully adhered. In terms of participating journalists, these were by far the most successful games until 1964 (with) ... 700 foreign journalists from 593 foreign media ... 15 wire services (and) ... 41 radio stations (which) ... reached an estimated 300 million radio listeners. (Kruger 2004: 44–5)

To a certain extent the Berlin Olympics brought forward, by thirty years, both McLuhan's dictum about the media being the message (1997) and

Debord's notion of the society of the spectacle (1983), but it's probably more accurate to say that it merely presaged those developments. The Second World War meant that attention and resources were shifted elsewhere, and it wasn't until Tokyo in 1964 that the Olympic Games produced a media event of comparable range or complexity. Moreover the integration of sport into the media–business nexus was developing very unevenly. In America and in sports such as boxing, baseball and horseracing it was well advanced, to the extent of being naturalized. In Europe the situation varied depending on the sport, but generally the media involved itself in the promotion, marketing and sponsorship of popular sporting events, competitions and teams: the Tour de France cycle race, which was organized for and by newspaper interests, is a case in point. On the other hand, British athletics, rugby, tennis and cricket remained relatively disdainful of the media, while soccer and rugby league were more accommodating.

CONCLUSION

We made the point earlier that the nascent Olympic movement was split, to some extent, between the more conservative factions and associations influenced by public school-style elitism, and those groups favouring Coubertin's internationalism and/as humanism; but in some ways these two positions were variants on a single theme – which was that sport was inherently valuable of and for itself. That theme may have been mediated by slightly different political agendas and contexts, but it remained a constant, even an article of faith. Consequently the Olympic movement, with its emphasis and insistence on its Greek heritage, amateurism, fair play and participation, coupled with its ability to put on a global sporting event that allowed nations to represent themselves on a world stage, carved out a particularly significant place for itself both within the field and in the wider socio-cultural domain. Similar, if less inflated, roles and forms of capital accrued to other sports, activities and events within the field at a global (the soccer World Cup), international (the Ashes cricket series, Wimbledon, the Libertadores Cup) and national (the Tour de France, the FA Cup Final, the World Series) levels. But as the popularity and status of sport increased, it became more attractive to the media, business and the field of politics. In the following chapters we will look in some detail at how the field of sport was transformed through its growing involvement with these three important cultural fields.

6 Sport, the Media and Spectatorship

INTRODUCTION

In our previous chapter we suggested that the 1936 Berlin Olympics presaged a development which is by now very familiar to us – the integration (in some areas, incorporation) of sport into the field of the media. This sport–media nexus has been the most significant factor in the transformation, from the second half of the twentieth century onward, of the field of sport and its practices: it has brought about the worldwide popularization of (some) games to new and wider demographics; changed the way players are perceived, treated and paid; redefined how spectators see and experience games, and indeed what we understand by the notion of spectatorship; and exerted a considerable influence over the rules, fixture lists, organizational structures and even the survival or sustainability of individual sports. In this chapter we will provide an historical and analytical account of this development, and consider how sport has negotiated the logics, imperatives, discourses and technologies of the mass media.

In *Power Play: Sport, the Media, and Popular Culture* Raymond Boyle and Richard Haynes make reference to literature of and about sport stretching back to the eighteenth century (2000: 24), including Strutt's *The Sports and Pastimes of the People of England*, as well as newspaper, magazine and journal accounts of cricket, racing and boxing. They point out, however, that:

> Sport was very marginal to the news agenda of the respectable press of the late eighteenth century and the early nineteenth. The cost of producing daily or weekly newsprint ... meant that sport could not compete for space in a copy-scarce environment. Even the cheap journalism of the radical press, which by the 1830s challenged the ... respectable press, as well as appealing to a predominantly working-class audience, could not find room for urban recreations.

Instead a wholly separate sporting press emerged to cater for genteel interests in horse-racing, prize-fighting and blood-sports. (25)

Basically up until the middle of the nineteenth century British journalism's coverage of sport was limited and inconsistent: sporting events might be mentioned in the social pages if they were patronized by royalty or significant members of the aristocracy; and newspapers provided "an occasional sports page" (Guttmann 1986: 85) that reported on important sporting events such as race meetings and county, MCC and public school cricket matches. There were, however, specialist publications (*The Sporting Magazine* and *Sporting Life*, and in the United States the *American Farmer* and *The Spirit of the Times*) and dailies (*Bell's Life in London*) that not only advertised fixtures and printed results and rules, but actively participated in discussions about sporting issues such as cricketing debates about the merits or otherwise of professionalism, changes to the LBW rule, and the legality of bowling actions.

A closer and more active relationship developed in the late nineteenth century, facilitated by the British Education Act of 1870 that "helped produce a new reading public" (Horne *et al.* 1999: 162); and by advances in communication technology and transport such as the use of the telegraph, which "reinvigorated off-course betting on horse-racing, enabling sporting newspapers to develop a national average from the transmission of racing odds and results ... to an expectant working-class betting market" (Boyle and Haynes 2000: 26). Specialist sporting magazines and other publications made their appearance (*Wisden* in 1864, *Athletic News* in 1875, the *Shooting Times* in 1882, *Horse and Hound* in 1884 (Boyle and Haynes 2000: 26–7), and by the 1890s there were regular sporting sections in daily newspapers in the USA, Britain and continental Europe.

THE SPORT–MEDIA NEXUS

As well as providing more detailed and wider coverage of sport, newspapers took on a more active role within the field. In Britain newspapers regularly provided detailed results, tip sheets and pools competitions for soccer, and sponsored and/or promoted events such as the Wimbledon tennis championships, prestigious horseracing events and golfing tournaments. In the USA newspapers promoted college football and baseball; regularly provided separate sections for racing results and baseball box-scores with their increasingly sophisticated statistical information; and sometimes took more interest in events such as the John L. Sullivan and James J. Corbett world title fight than they did in presidential elections (Isenberg 1997: 233). In France the sports newspaper *L'Auto* (later *L'Equipe*), under the editorship of Henri Desgrange, created the Tour de France cycling race, which "exerted an instant fascination on the French public" and "became one of the great sporting events in the world" (Holt 1980: 96–7). It was integrated into the daily lives of the communities through which it passed, and became associated with or emblematic of everything from summer holidays and the ruggedness and beauty of the French countryside to the masculinity of the hardy French peasant and ethnic and national pride. The Tour "found a place in the national mythology of France and was followed anxiously by persons not generally interested in sport as well as by those who were" (Holt 1980: 101). This provided Desgrange and his newspaper with new readers, a development that fed back into and further boosted this incipient sport–media–business nexus:

> Newspapers founded races over which they tried to establish exclusive rights as part of a drive to increase circulation and bring in greater advertising revenue. The major manufacturers encouraged newspapers to promote cycling by offering papers lucrative inducements, and they often subsidised races themselves. (Holt 1980: 101)

The privileged position that sport had come to occupy (at least in Britain) in the social field, largely attributable to its upper-class and public school connections, was accentuated once sporting events, rules, conflicts and stars became daily news for a newly literate mass audience. Sport helped provide millions of daily readers for publications such as the *Sportsman*, *Sporting Life*, the *Daily Mail* (in Britain), *Le Sport*, *Le Velo*, *Sport in Wort*, the *Allgemeine Zeitung*, *L'Equipe* (Europe), *The Police Gazette*, the *New York Herald* and the *New York Times* (USA). These publications reciprocated by disposing their readers to play cricket, soccer and baseball; cycle and row; gamble on horseraces and boxing matches; buy sporting equipment; and most significantly, identify with and barrack for local teams or (media-promoted) sports stars. In short, the sport–media nexus helped to turn a large proportion and a much wider demographic of the population of Britain, the United States and Europe into sports players, spectators and fans with an "insatiable thirst for sports news" (Guttmann 1986: 85).

How, and to what extent, did this development impact on the field of sport? We made the point, in previous chapters, that initially the field of sport was largely participatory and elitist. The upper and middle classes trained and transformed themselves through action and activity, which helped distinguish them from the lower classes. It also worked, within those class factions, to differentiate the 'right sort of person' from the effete, the soft, the thinker, the sensualist and the observer. In its incipient stages modern sport and its administrators, rules, discourses and practices strongly reflected and reproduced this world-view; by the end of the century, however, the value, functions and demographics of sports participation had changed. We referred to the work of Christian groups and other reformers who tried to improve the physical and moral health of the British working class by promoting and facilitating participation in individual exercise and team sport, and much the same was true of Europe and the United States. In the United States the impact of "immigration, industrialization, family disruption ... and deepening class divisions" produced a health reform movement dedicated to "renovating the spiritual and physical condition of Americans" (Borish 1997: 95–6). Moreover the utility of sport and exercise could be justified on economic grounds, since "The cost of parks would be far less than the cost of jails, prisons, and police used in repressing wasteful indulgences like liquor and gambling" (Riess 1997a: 154). Newspapers not only concurred – they actively advanced the debate. A *New York Times* editorial of 1875, for instance, lauds the usefulness and popularity of Central Park while suggesting that:

> means needed to be contrived for carrying the masses of the people from the crowded tenement-house quarters, cheaply to these charming scenes ... What the laborers and the children of the poor and the tired business men most need are simple, pleasant country scenes, with solitary rambles and quiet walks. (Riess 1997a: 141–2)

SPORT AND SPECTATORSHIP

In the United States, much more than was the case in Britain, Europe or the British Empire, professional and even college sports increasingly produced themselves as forms of entertainment with a strong spectatorial inflection. The emergence of a form of spectatorship tied to or associated with the modern sport–media nexus was without doubt a profound development, but it was not without its antecedents. The Roman and Byzantine games were set up as entertainment for groups who had a highly developed and formalized sense of their roles and modes of behaviour. There also tended to be a passionate and enduring sense of identification with a colour that was not necessarily predicated on class, racial, ethnic or even geographical factors. The blue and the green factions, for instance, sat in allocated places; engaged in chant-and-response sessions with each other (as well as the reds and the whites); were 'orchestrated' (in both their chanting and communications with prominent senators, officials or the emperor) by a designated and specialized hierarchy; and more generally shared an ethos which informed their understanding of the games and their own role as spectators.

This notion of spectatorship is much closer to contemporary sport than is the case with the groups who watched folk football, or even boxing, football or baseball crowds of the first half of the nineteenth century. Consider, for example, the following account of the behaviour of fifteen thousand baseball spectators at a game, in 1860, between the Atlantics and the Excelsiors:

> The excitement among the baseball fraternity was intense before the climatic encounter, as rumours circulated that the Excelsiors would not be allowed to win a close contest. During the early play one of the Atlantics agitated part of the crowd by refusing to yield immediately to an umpire's call ... Captain Joseph Leggett of the Excelsiors warned the spectators that his team would withdraw if the hooting continued. Members of the Atlantics then appealed to their supporters to permit the game to continue, as 100 policemen tried to restrain the unruly onlookers. But when the roughs increased their yelling and abuse of the umpire and the Excelsiors, Leggett ordered his players off the field. As they left, a large crowd pursued them. (Kirsche 1997: 103)

This report refers to spectators, but also to a fraternity, crowd, supporters, onlookers and roughs: George B. Kirsche, a (contemporary) writer/historian, is trying to make sense of historical activities using a variety of terms, none of which entirely fit in or sit easily with the action being described. Kirsche goes on to explain that due to economic reasons, the people who usually attended baseball games prior the 1860s were upper and middle class, but when this started to change after the Civil War attempts were made to exclude or at least limit the attendance of the lower classes. The reasons for this were that working-class behaviour at sporting contests was associated with endemic violence, crime (assaults and pick-pocketing), drunkenness and gambling, and gang and sectarian rivalries. These factors either required the host club to go to a great deal of trouble to maintain order or, if this wasn't forthcoming, rendered each game liable to interruption if the wrong side was winning. The potential for disruption was also exacerbated by a high level of corruption (involving gambling on games), widespread intoxication, the inadequacy of enclosures meant to keep non-paying spectators out, and the proximity of the crowd to the field of play coupled with the absence of barriers preventing them from invading the field. Kirsche describes troublemakers as "an unruly minority" (110), but it is clear that at professional baseball games throughout the nineteenth century sections of the crowd "drank, cheered, heckled, gambled ... (and) fought in the grandstands" (110), and occasionally invaded the playing field.

The *Clipper* newspaper knew the remedy to the "spirit of faction ... in which the foreign element of our immense metropolitan population, and their native offspring, especially, delights to indulge" lay in the "self-control of contending clubs and parties, and in a strict adherence to the rules that guide the actions of a man of honor and a gentleman" (Kirsche 1997: 109). In other words the ethnic lower classes, under the combined influence of what Elias would call the civilizing influence and sportization, needed to learn to behave like gentlemen. The group Kirsche refers to, and whose behaviour he describes at the Atlantics–Excelsiors game, are not (proper) spectators in any modern sense precisely because they don't know anything about, and aren't interested in, the protocols and forms of civilized and market-driven spectatorship. They're a lot of things – a crowd, onlookers, supporters and roughs – and they move fluidly and capriciously in and out of and across these categories. They're also (potentially) a mob, and whereas mobs look to intervene, the (modern) spectator intervenes to look.

We made the point that the culture of Roman and Byzantine circus/games crowds can be distinguished from their pre-modern counterparts because of the highly formalized and durable culture that contextualized and animated their activities. The group that rioted at the Atlantics–Excelsior game, in comparison, may have identified with a team on the day or even across seasons, but its behaviour can be seen as relatively contingent, ephemeral and unpredictable, likely to be set off in one direction or another by gambling losses, intoxication or random incitements. At this point of time and place there simply wasn't enough of a developed culture of spectatorship for the crowd to be imagined into existence, week in and out, as a consistently homogeneous identity and set of practices. Violence really isn't the key differential here: Roman and Byzantine crowds could (and not infrequently did) transform themselves into mobs that roamed the streets setting fire to buildings and beating up or killing other supporters, unpopular officials and ethnic minorities – but in a peculiarly modern way. For the members of the Blues and Greens, much as for certain sections of Real Madrid, Lazio, Leeds United, Glasgow Rangers and other soccer clubs, violence was both part of the attraction of spectatorship-as-supporter, and an extension of that culture. Partisans at a mime-dancing shows, for instance, often entered into a ritualized relationship with some of the more popular dancers, who deliberately (by miming particular nefarious actions of a rival, public official, or the emperor) egged them on: mob violence, in this case, was really the final act of the performance, much as laying waste to shops, beating up locals and/or engaging in (pre-arranged over the internet) pitched battles with opposing supporters is considered by certain factions (such as Real Madrid's notorious Plus Ultra group) to be a salient aspect of the game-as-event.

The commercialization of baseball after the Civil War boosted attendances and newspaper coverage, increased admission prices, attracted a wider demographic, spread professionalism, and helped standardize rules and equipment – but it didn't immediately "bring any drastic changes in the behaviour of audiences" (Kirsche 1997: 109). These factors certainly predisposed and facilitated a more formalized culture of spectatorship, but the real catalyst was something more profound and far-reaching – the careful, deliberate, thorough and co-ordinated integration of important sporting events, competitions and teams (at first in the United States, but Britain and Europe gradually followed) into the logics and culture of the cognate and closely networked fields of the media, entertainment and business. Robin Lester provides one example (focusing on the activities of athletic entrepreneur Amos Stagg during period 1895–1905) of this process, and explains how it was effected as a kind of cultural transformation:

> The most significant development during the period was the rise of the spectator – the widespread acceptance and use of the Chicago football enterprise by the students, faculty, alumni of the university community and by the larger civic community ... The university became very successful in selling its athletic product and even of applying monopolistic principles ... The 'windy city' newspaper boosters maintained their civic reputation with unsupportable claims for the Stagg men. The journalists themselves were a prime market for the game, even as they became the chief salesmen ... Boosterism came full circle in 1902 when the first 'Gridiron Fest' was sponsored by the Chicago Press Club. Coaches, athletic managers, football officials, and players joined the propagandists in the formal unification of the press and the new intercollegiate football industry ... Chicago was a limited football marketplace in the early 1890s because few Chicagoans knew the game either as players or spectators. The public interest in the game picked up when the sport was introduced into secondary schools and (because of) ... persistent publicity which argued that the honor of the collegiate and civic community was at stake on the Maroon gridiron ... Pre-game rallies, school songs, football banquets and receptions, celebrity bonfires and parades – all these spectatorial accoutrements to the Chicago football industry were begun, developed, and refined during the period to the degree that they changed little over the next decades. (1997: 128–9)

We suggested that our pre-modern baseball crowd was unlikely to have been consistently and comprehensively 'imagined into existence': the reference here is to Anderson's notion of imagined communities (1993), which suggests that disparate groups are interpellated and act as members of a community via a chain of cultural representations and apparatuses, in particular those disseminated through or associated with the media. Sport has been both instrumental and fundamental with regard to this process at numerous times and places: we can think of Celtic and Rangers vis-à-vis religious and ethnic identity; Barcelona and Athletic Bilbao regarding ethnicity-as-nationalism; Boca Juniors and River Plate at the level of class; and Flamengo and Fluminense in terms of race. What Lester is referring to with the example of the University of Chicago football team is something a little more complex, however, because the process entails the simultaneous production of a communal identity and/as a commodity. In other words the identity-as-process is utterly social and inalienable ('the honour of the collegiate and civic community is at stake'), but the community-as-brand, the spectators and supporters who testify to and embody it, and the various rituals and signs through which it is manifested and articulated (sweatshirts, rallies, banquets and the game itself), are commodities, the result of entrepreneurial activity, marketing, media advertising and a concerted public relations campaign.

This looks like a contradiction – (sporting) identity as simultaneously both inalienable and a commodity – but it is perfectly explicable if we make use of Arjun Appadurai's insight that the commodity is not so much a thing as a situation or phase:

> Let us approach commodities as things in a certain situation, a situation that can characterize many different kinds of thing, at different points in their social lives. This means looking at the commodity potential of all things rather than searching fruitlessly for the magic distinction between commodities and other sorts of things. It also means breaking significantly with the production-dominated Marxian view of the commodity and focusing on its total trajectory from production, through exchange/distribution, to consumption. But how do we define the commodity situation? I propose that the commodity situation in the social life of any 'thing' be defined as the situation in which its exchangeability (past, present, or future) for some thing is its socially relevant feature. (Appadurai 1988: 13)

The value of this definition is that it renders irrelevant the question of whether sport-as-communal identity was colonized or produced by the media in tandem with business; and concomitantly it also means that spectators at sporting events are partaking of a form of social life and activity even when the subjectivities on which this is predicated are entirely manufactured. So the crowd that gathered to watch and cheer on Chicago, sang and screamed, wore the sweatshirts, waved the flags, responded to scores and referees' decisions, idolized and identified with players, and most importantly watched and experienced the game as if it were a crucial part of their lives, had been carefully taught and disposed (through newspaper reports and articles, by talking to regulars, and by watching at games and rallies and learning, unconsciously, how and when to move and shout) to show and experience passion. This is the inalienable and the production–distribution–consumption (not to mention marketing and advertising) nexus all rolled into one self-perpetuating process; and it is also what effectively distinguishes this new spectacle from the Roman circuses and pre-modern baseball games. The former were not entirely removed from the commodity situation (for instance, they entertained the unemployed and contributed to the standing of the emperor, or aristocratic or wealthy patrons), while the latter was clearly integrated into the logics and apparatuses of entrepreneurship and the market. However, while Roman crowds functioned as consistently interpellated communities (behaviour was ritualized and carefully scripted, subjectivities recognized and durable), it wasn't a commodity *per se*, nor was it the departure point for new forms of production, distribution and consumption. The pre-modern baseball crowd was neither homogeneous nor easily interpellated on any consistent basis, and therefore couldn't function as a commodity; if anything it was a kind of anti-commodity, since its ephemeral and volatile nature threatened or vitiated the commodity status of the game itself.

What's missing from both these pre-modern examples (and what characterizes the growth of spectatorship of the kind found with the University of Chicago football programme) is a mechanism that teaches and disseminates identities and dispositions beyond the limitations of time and place, and then integrates them into an ongoing cycle and logic of commoditization. In short what is lacking is the media and its ability to transform its (literate) audiences into sports spectators with a passionate and/or enduring attachment to the events at hand, which in itself becomes part of the process of production/commoditization. This is the real significance of the media to the field of sport at the end of the nineteenth century – it creates not just games as spectacles, but more importantly spectators and/as fans. We can see just how significant this innovation has become: whereas at the beginning of modern professional sport the value of the game as commodity is largely attested to by the crowd it draws, by the end of the twentieth century this is reversed – the value of the spectators as commodity (television viewers, passionate spectators/fans that create noise and atmosphere) is to some extent predicated on the game (hence the idea of television delivering up Super Bowl or World Cup final audiences to advertisers).

SPECTATORS AND SPORTS LITERACY

In *Sports Spectators*, one of the few detailed studies devoted to the history and theory of sports spectatorship, Allen Guttmann offers the following definitions of, and means of differentiating between, the two terms:

> The sports spectator is anyone who views a sporting event, either in situ or through visual media such as film or television. In their social roles, the fans who follow sports in the newspapers and magazines or on the radio are certainly similar to those who sit in the ballpark or flip on the TV, but a conceptual line has to be drawn somewhere between those who experience a sports event 'fully' and those whose experience is partial ... The term fan here refers

to the emotionally committed 'consumer' of sports events. The terms overlap but are obviously not identical. In practice most fans are spectators and most spectators are fans, but it is logically possible to be one and not the other. (1986: 5–6)

This distinction may have been tenable at the beginning of the twentieth century, before the advent of television and film newsreels, but even then it is limited – we can at best refer to genres of spectators and spectatorship. People who attended games, followed and barracked for teams all over the country and paid for the privilege each week, certainly constituted one genre, but they weren't the same species as the person who stopped by a village green or the local playing field to catch a few moments of a game of cricket or soccer. If anything those paying spectators have less in common with the casual spectator as they have with the newspaper readers who rarely if ever go to a professional game, but follow scores, accounts of matches, news of injuries and photographs of the action with a similar kind of fervour. To limit the notion of the spectator to 'in situ' presence or mediated access to a game is to leave out or ignore the fact that to be a sports fan is necessarily to have some kind of visual connection with the action and/or players. When we read and immerse ourselves in newspaper or internet news site reports of sporting contests, we (actively) engage with the game on some kind of visual level. To read an account of how the winning goal was headed into the net by the centre forward flinging him- or herself horizontally between defenders to meet a ball cut-back by a winger, or how the opening bat hooked a six, requires that we imagine the action (based on our inter-textual knowledge of the game and players) into existence – and that we become spectators.

This form of spectatorship is generically different to what happens when we attend a game as a fan, which is not the same experience as casual in situ spectatorship, which needs to be distinguished from watching the same game live on television or even listening to it on the radio or over the internet, which isn't exactly the same as watching a replay of the game. We can explore this issue a little more by way of reference to Guttmann's suggestion that we need to differentiate along conceptual lines "between those who experience a sports event 'fully' and those whose experience is partial" (1986: 6). Guttmann presumes that 'in situ' presence equals fullness, but the definition is then extended so that any kind of technology-mediated visual apprehension 'stands in for' presence. Now the subjective nature of the process of visualization has been sufficiently attested to (see Schirato and Webb 2004) that we can quickly move beyond the notion that to be present at or have access to a representation of a game does not mean that we all see the same things. At a basic level, watching a game live and on television are two separate visual processes that produce completely different visual texts – the frames, levels of detail, commentary, the availability of replays and the interaction of other spectators all dispose and influence our 'editing' of the action.

Guttmann's definition of a spectator is predicated on the notion/ possibility of a subjective response to an 'authentic' representation: after all, if we watch a game on television, we can claim that we see what really happened, rather than what we imagined into existence from newspaper reports. There are three (inter-related) objections to this position, however. First, the process of visualization is always necessarily a (selective) form of semiosis: the human visual apparatus never captures the world – it decodes it. Second, this act/process of decoding is essentially the same for all semiotic systems and mediums: it doesn't matter whether we are referring to colour, movement or shapes or words on a page, what we are doing is textualizing and representing the world. Third, what we see, even when we're 'fully present' at a game, is always filtered through the various (predominantly media) inter-texts that teach us about, and help us become literate with regard to, the rules, rituals, techniques and actions of a game. Even if we were to give ground regarding the issue of authentic and/or subjective vision, it could be pointed out that newspapers contain 'authentic' photographs that are viewed after the event, and contemporary computer technology allows for digital images of games-in-progress to be made available and downloaded within a time delay comparable to that of many supposedly 'live' transmissions. In any case, Guttmann never specifies whether spectatorship has a temporal dimension to it: presumably, watching a game 'in situ' is more or less the same thing as watching a television replay the next day (or weeks later, for that matter).

This complex relation between visualization, representation, 'authentic mediation' and sports spectatorship became even more relevant and accentuated from the moment the media, in an attempt to take advantage of the popularity of sport and the enthusiasm/passion of team supporters, committed to 'bringing the game' to the fan. From the late nineteenth century on spectators increasingly came to see through, and were disposed by, newspaper reports about and representations and evaluations of individual sports (the status of cricket within English culture), competitions (the significance of the Ashes series, the England–Scotland soccer match, and the Roses cricket games between Lancashire and Yorkshire) and players (W.G. Grace, the 'Demon' Spofforth and C.B. Fry as cult figures). How precisely did this burgeoning newspaper coverage of sport help facilitate, promote and naturalize sports spectatorship at what we might term a technical level? The imperative to 'bring the game to the fans' required newspapers to take it upon themselves to teach their readers about sporting competitions, players, categories, genres, discourses, practices, activities, rules, rhythms and traditions (if they existed – if not, they had to be invented, as was the case with the numerous 'traditional football rivalries' that came into being in the late nineteenth or early twentieth centuries). In short, attentive readers acquired literacy with regard to the field at a micro- (distinguishing between rugby union and league, understanding the difference between a 'centre half' and a 'centre forward', making sense of the statistic of 'earned run average') and macro-level (appreciating the ethos of sport).

When we refer to literacy here we are using the term in the sense of a wider cultural literacy, a concept that implies "not just familiarity with a body of knowledge; it also presupposes an understanding of how to think and see in a manner that is appropriate to the imperatives and contexts of the moment" (Schirato and Webb 2004: 18). An untutored and illiterate eye that tries to take in what is happening in a rugby maul or the coming together of the offensive and defensive lines during a running play in a NFL game will see nothing – or at least nothing that makes sense. We pointed out that the human visual apparatus doesn't give us the world in an unmediated form – it effectively decodes it. When that apparatus has to deal with considerable detail (numerous bodies rushing at speed in different directions, a ball flying through the air) it simply can't take everything in: what it does is to extrapolate from a combination of details apprehended and what is known. The result is sometimes what we could call an 'authentic fiction': we see correctly (the ball was caught; the player was onside, or did get past the crease before the stumps were broken), but we didn't actually see it happen at all – effectively we imagined it. This explains why a far more experienced squash referee will be able to clearly distinguish if a player has failed to retrieve the ball before it has bounced a second time, while a novice with considerably better eyesight will simply 'not see' the second bounce. The older and more literate referee takes the detail at hand (position of the player, distance to the ball, speed, angle of approach), reads it and constructs a credible visual text (the racquet connecting with the ball a split-second after a second bounce), while the younger referee reads a foreign language.

As a part of this process of producing enthusiasts and/as literate sports spectators, newspapers not only provided wider coverage of sport – they also included increasingly complex statistical information about sports such as baseball and cricket. Baseball in particular has a strong statistical inflection, sufficient for Allen Guttmann to suggest that an understanding and appreciation of the game requires not so much literacy as "numeracy":

> baseball was from the start marked by quantification and by the proliferation of records that quantification alone makes possible ... Half the drama of the game (the invisible half, which European spectators cannot perceive) lies in the

calculation of the fan who understands the significance of a 3–2 count and knows that a player batting .347 can bring in the tying run from second base … The quantified action, which includes four balls, three strikes, three outs, and nine innings, leads to an abstract world of batting averages, fielding averages, earned run averages, and all the other spectral numbers that haunt the ballpark, flicker at the side of the televised images, fill the columns of *The Sporting News*, and come to rest, finally, in the hallowed pages of *The Baseball Encyclopaedia*. (1988: 54)

Newspapers printed box-scores that, as well as taking up considerable space and to some extent necessitating the development of a separate sports section, disposed spectators to see in an increasingly detailed and attentive manner. This numerically inflected 'way of seeing' is reinscribed in every newspaper report which informs us that a pitcher's ERA is 2.03, rises to 3.41 when facing left-handed hitters and to .395 after eighty balls or more had been thrown; or that a batter's average is .302, but .340 over the last month, with an on-base percentage of .381, but leads the league in double-plays. Baseball games are read, seen and narrated within and through relations that are posited between numbers, statistics and contexts: one out, bases loaded, bottom of the ninth innings, pitching team leading by the only run of the game, with the possibility of the pitcher throwing a perfect game (no hits or runs or walks). History beckons (perfect games are very rare), but a relieving pitcher probably makes more sense (statistically). In other words, would the manager look at the numbers-as-situation and decide that, no matter how well his starter was pitching, this was not a good match-up – or give him his shot at history, and leave him in the game? How does the pitcher deal with the psychological pressure associated with the 'truth' of his poor record against left-handers late in the game, or the batter with his history of hitting into a double play that would end the innings?

This imperative, on the part of newspapers and other media, to educate spectators was a requisite part of getting and holding the attention of the public: readers needed to be caught up by, drawn into, and care passionately about, games and teams and players and competitions and issues, and the more they knew and saw, the easier it was to effect and maintain this attentive and affective response. In short, media representations of sport – whether it was a book about a famous player or event, a pamphlet promoting an upcoming game, or a newspaper article describing how and why a match was won and lost – had to be narrated in such a dramatic and affecting manner that the reader vicariously saw and experienced the contest. Consider the following excerpt from Burt Standish's 'Dick Merriwell Saves the Game', a 1909 account of a Yale-Brown college football match:

By the game with Brown, Dick Merriwell developed an attack of malaria … Brown had a fine team and it fought hard … (they) opened the second half with a substitute fullback, a giant, who weighed at least 230 pounds. This man Perkins ... battered and beat men down before him, and left them stretched like dying soldiers ... in less than five minutes he had injured three or four forwards, and sent them from the field ... The team showed no signs of wavering, not a symptom of fear. And yet, if this slaughter kept up ... the blue might go down in defeat ... A few of them took note of what was occurring on the side lines ... They saw old Bill Fullerton kneeling on one knee, send out substitute after substitute. They saw Dick Merriwell approach him thrice and appeal to him. They saw Fullerton shake his head ... Suddenly there was a pause. Still another Yale man lay stretched on the damp sod ... Go ahead, cried old Bill suddenly: 'If anybody can stop him, you're the man' ... Again Perkins plunged. But the new right half-back flung himself headlong, squeezed the giant's knee, held him tight, and stopped him there ... Dick Merriwell slammed Perkins to the ground with such fury that it seemed as if the earth must quiver from the shock. Then both the giant and Merriwell were sent stretched silent and motionless side by side ... With the stop of Perkins the tide turned. From that time forward Yale has her own way, even though Brown fought stubbornly to the last ditch. (Standish 1997: 311–12)

This text can be characterized in a number of ways – as affecting, melodramatic and hyperbolic – but what is of particular interest is how it breaks the games down into a collection of vignettes or even tableaux. The descriptions-as-narrative are intensely visual, not so much cinematic or televisual as photographic and/or pictorial. Standish has effectively arranged a series of scenes – each represented in an overblown, almost mock-heroic style – side-by-side, without recourse to overt editorializing or narrating. But because the story is, at a generic level, so familiar and predictable, it is relatively easy for the reader to make the appropriate connections and evaluations. This pictorial and allegorical style of writing (in the first vignette the giant stands, clearly threatening, ominous and powerful; in the next the bodies lay scattered, like a scene from a Civil War battlefield; then the coach kneels, as he sends fresh players to their doom, etc.) has two major functions. First, it mediates without any apparent distancing effect: it invites and facilitates a visualizing of bodies, movement, expressions and relationships. Second and concomitantly, because of its allegorical nature we are left in no doubt as to how to experience and respond to the text: we are disposed to look and attend, and to throw ourselves, emotionally, into the game-as-scenes.

At this point it's useful to return to the three main propositions regarding spectators and fans that Guttmann puts forward in *Sports Spectators*. First, the sports spectator is "anyone who views a sporting event, either in situ or through visual media such as film or television". Second, fans are "emotionally committed 'consumers' of sports events". Third, fans who "follow sports in the newspapers and magazines or on the radio" are similar to spectators, but "a conceptual line has to be drawn somewhere between those

who experience a sports event 'fully' and those whose experience is partial"
(1986: 5–6). We've already established that the first, and to some extent the
third, propositions aren't tenable except in the most limited and generic way:
at the level of text and tectonics the distinctions made between taking in and
experiencing a game 'in situ', on television, via photographs or even through
a written text are arbitrary rather than fundamental. The second proposition
about fans being consumers of sport is useful, however, as is Guttmann's
very practical observation that the two terms "overlap but are obviously
not identical. In practice most fans are spectators and most spectators
are fans" (6).

How can we make sense of these terms as they apply at/to the level of
practice? It seems clear that the close relationship between sport and the
media from the late nineteenth century on produced genres and regimes of
subjectivity corresponding to the (closely related) terms/categories sports
spectator and sports fan. Many of the spectators who attended the
University of Chicago football games at the end of the nineteenth
century, for instance, were doubtlessly the products of a pedagogy-
as-inculcation. They had not only learned, largely from and through the
media, about the game, the team and the players; like the English public
school students playing rugby or cricket, those spectators lost and found
themselves in the ethos, the activity and the occasion of sport. They lost
themselves in the sense that they could throw off their other various everyday and 'serious' subjectivities (Irish-American, catholic, clerk, father, sister,
soldier, student, businessperson) in favour of this sometimes passionate and
rather otherworldly attachment. They found themselves in the sense that
this attachment didn't disappear, or wasn't neatly sequestered until and after
game time. Rather, it provided them with an ethos (tied in with notions of
fair play, loyalty, struggle, self-sacrifice, endurance and overcoming) and a
set of social relations and networks (with regard to other spectators and
alumni) that often carried over into the wider social field, and which manifested itself in the consumption of commodities (sweatshirts, souvenirs,
attendance at booster events) associated with the team. They were 'emotionally committed consumers of sports' whose (visual) experience of the game
was filtered through or at least inflected by that emotional attachment.

The subject who has incorporated the ethos, values and logics of a field
has an entirely different relationship to the activities and events in/of the
field than that of a visitor or passer by. Sports fans become
literate with regard to the field precisely because they consider that
the 'game' of watching and seeing with a knowledgeable and cultivated eye
is worth playing. The non-sports spectator who accompanies a friend to a
baseball game, watches cricket on television while channel-hopping, down-
loads photographs of bikini-clad beach volleyball players, or reads newspaper

accounts of a football riot can be differentiated from sports spectators not just by a lack of technical expertise ('what is a knuckleball?') and overall literacy ('why does the bowling team have eleven players, and the batting side only two?'); even more importantly, they just can't see the point of the expenditure of time and effort. Similarly, someone watching as a business executive (who is not a sports fan) sees the game or team as an economic commodity: the activity or thing is seen, but not on its own terms. Sports fans, on the other hand, take the game 'at its word': they are, in their acts and roles of spectatorship, simply testifying to, as well as extending and manifesting, the field and its articulation of its own self worth. In Bourdieu's terms, they believe, and see it as if, 'it's worth the candle' (2000).

For some time the field of sport didn't quite believe in, or at least was highly suspicion of, spectators and spectatorship. The modern sporting ethos that developed in English public schools was strongly participatory, and looked upon spectatorship as almost antithetical to sport; in the nineteenth century being a spectator connoted not just passivity, but also idleness and laziness, and these meanings became even more accentuated with the rise of muscular Christianity. Of course for schoolmasters, ex-pupils and the 'right sort of people', watching a rugby game or cricket match between, say, Eton and Winchester was a perfectly proper and justifiable activity – and of another order to what was happening at the University of Chicago or a professional soccer game between Celtic and Rangers. This difference was particularly manifest in the forms of behaviour and relations-to-the game that characterized northern and southern crowds who followed rugby union in the late nineteenth century. Rugby became popular from the 1870s on, particularly in Yorkshire: it had become "a focus for outpourings of civic pride" (Collins 1998: 40) and was capable of attracting larger crowds than comparable soccer games. This increase in attendances at northern games was accompanied, however, by behaviour that scandalized southern clubs, rugby officials and newspaper reporters and editors. Acts of violence were sometimes committed against referees, opposing teams and supporters, as well as members of the general public, and there were other perceived concomitant evils such as professionalism and gambling. Much of the concern, however, was directed at the improprieties of (largely working-class) crowds and their relation to the game:

> Without exception, judgements about the behaviour of crowds, or more particularly the working-class sections of crowds, were made by middle-class commentators, and it is noticeable that, certainly in the period leading up to 1886, the vast majority of the criticisms of crowd behaviour was not about violence but about the language and enthusiasm of working-class spectators. 'When I say that the home spectators were simply a howling, surging, abusive mob, I don't exaggerate one whit' wrote a reporter sent to cover a Castleford versus

Bradford match, although he was unable to report any violence before, during or after the match. As one might expect, the imagery of the 'mob' loomed large for those unused to, or afraid of, working-class people gathering in their thousands ... the sharp contrast in the behaviour of the classes was seen as a disincentive to middle-class players and spectators. 'If "mob law" is permitted to run riot on the football field, however great the provocation, the pastime will become no game for gentlemen', wrote the *Yorkshire Post* sternly in 1886. (Collins 1998: 48–9)

What disqualified those less-than-gentlemanly Yorkshire crowds from being considered as anything more than a mob was their inability or refusal to conform to a proper regime of behaviour – one in keeping with the values and discourses of the field. Rugby spectators were meant to watch the game with what Bourdieu would call 'interested disinterestedness' (1991a): they might see and experience things as supporters, but they were not to overstep the mark or lose control. The rabid and potentially riotous (working-class) crowd, motivated and animated by mindless partisanship or gambling interests, was the spectator equivalent of the "much dreaded and detested professional footballer – the man who plays not for love and honour but for gain" (Collins 1998: 57). The ethical imperative 'It's not about winning or losing, but how you play the game' applied equally to spectators: to care too much about whether your team won or not was to dissolve the game as an ethos and marker of distinction. This disassociation, particularly in Britain, between the field and its discourses (as formulated and articulated by the upper-middle-class, public school educated elites who oversaw its governance) on the one hand, and its increasing professionalized and spectator-driven practices and competitions, on the other, led to a split in the sport of rugby along professional–amateur and (largely) north–south lines in 1895, and the emergence of two separate sports – staunchly amateur and (largely) upper-class rugby union and professional (and very much working-class) rugby league.

The situation was handled less dramatically in cricket. The behaviour of crowds at pre-modern matches seems to have been not dissimilar to the Atlantics–Excelsiors game – violence was the exception, but not unknown; gambling, alcohol consumption and excessive partisanship could sometimes force play to be curtailed or abandoned; and there is little evidence to suggest that a cricket crowd thought of itself in those specific terms. This changed when cricket was adopted by, and came to be closely associated with, English public school-educated elites. For much of the last one hundred and forty years, cricket spectators – particularly in England – have tended to eschew forms of behaviour 'that aren't cricket': so demonstrativeness, excessive noise or zeal, violent actions or movements, abuse and mindless partisanship are usually frowned upon. The cricket spectator is interested less in winning and losing than in the 'game itself', which produces a polite, respectful, patient and relatively quiet attentiveness to minutiae and subtleties. This is manifested in a number of ways, for instance in the necessity of seeing and responding to a deceptively flighted leg break or a well executed late cut without regard to which side the player is on; or even more incomprehensibly (say, to a Chinese or Russian) in an appreciation of 'stoic inactivity', as when a player lets ball after ball go through to the keeper or offers a dead bat to everything. To watch a cricket game is to understand precisely what Bourdieu means when he refers to the field-specific inculcation of a bodily hexis (2000); spectators at a soccer match, for instance, will usually view an opposition goal as an unmitigated disaster, and react accordingly (either with stunned silence, or by directing abuse at the scorer or the defender at fault), but the sight of a cover drive sending the ball speeding to the boundary will bring the cricket spectator's hands together spontaneously – regardless of who has benefited.

Cricket spectators are disposed to see their sport as an ethical activity, and provocation offers no justification – control as/and the maintenance of form is all. Derek Birley refers to an incident during the Eton versus Harrow match of 1870 in which the same Lord Harris who proselytized the virtues of cricket in India shamelessly ran out a batsman who was "backing up too eagerly", thus incurring "a noisy expression of disapproval from the Harrow partisans" (2003: 113). The gentlemen of the MCC weren't quick to respond, but respond they did:

> Three years later the MCC issues a statement of pained disapproval at this 'unseemly conduct' of spectators, adding, 'Such scenes ... would not occur if the partisans of both schools were to assist the authorities in checking the immoderate expression at the conclusion of the match'. (2003: 113–14)

Cricket, perhaps more than any other sporting activity, enacts its distinction at the level of bodily hexis, simultaneously renouncing the idea of politics or interestedness in every sense while performing a pedagogy ('this is how a self-possessed, confident and reasonable person moves and acts') of exclusion ('you don't belong here – your body gives you away'). Bourdieu points out that there is there is a tendency for "the privileged classes to treat the body as an end in itself" (1991a: 371), with emphasis being placed either on "the intrinsic functioning of the body as an organism" or "on the appearance of the body as a perceptible configuration" (371); and clearly, cricket falls into the second category. Although the Australian batsman Don Bradman has the highest test batting average, whenever cricket writers and commentators refer to his exploits they do so with caveats that imply that his success was too driven and relentless – and lacked style. The famous cricketing journalist and author Neville Cardus, for instance, wrote that

"When Bradman passed 200 at Leeds I felt that my interest in his play might break out anew at the sight of one miscalculated stroke" (1934: 29). Discussing the less well-performed Ranjitsinhji, on the other hand, he employs an entirely different kind of discourse:

> Cricketers will never see the like of Ranjitsinhji; he was entirely original, and there is nothing in all the history and development of batsmanship with which we can compare him. His style was a remarkable insistence of the way a man can express personal genius in a game – nay, not only a personal genius but the genius of a whole race ... when he batted a strange light was seen for the first time on English fields ... It was lovely magic ... Ranji belonged to the land ... where beauty is subtle and not plain and unambiguous. (1934: 70)

Leaving aside the orientalist inflection, this and other descriptions of Ranji invariably emphasize the style and grace of his movements and shots; it wasn't the number of runs he scored that mattered, but the manner in which he accumulated them – hence the references to his genius, magic and 'strange light'. This kind of lyricism characterized cricketing journalism and book writing – and later both radio and television commentary – throughout the twentieth century, and helped dispose the cricket spectator to view the game with what Bourdieu (1995) would call an 'upside down' logic. What this means is that normally what we would understand as strong and influential logics and regimes of value – for instance, the capitalist value of capital accumulation – pervade and influence most fields; so regardless of whether we are talking about the fields of law, accountancy or architecture, receiving a high salary would constitute one form of positive capital – and it certainly wouldn't count against the person. There are fields, however, where this doesn't necessarily apply: in literature and art, for instance, achieving commercial success can be read and experienced as negative capital – along the lines of 'if everyone buys and likes your novel, it cant be very good'. In the field of sport, capital is usually tied in with measurable or valorized forms of success achieved within the rules of the game – scoring goals, winning competitions and breaking records. This is true of cricket to some extent, but the emphasis on style meant that sometimes and in certain places (particularly in the so-called 'golden age' of cricket at the turn of the century, and in southeast counties rather than, say, Yorkshire) runs scored in an ugly or cumbersome manner could be less admired than fewer runs scored in a more fluid, technically correct, subtle or elegant manner.

This preference for style and form over calculation and quantifiable profit was maintained, in England, until well into the twentieth century – setting cricket and cricket spectatorship apart from popular sports such as football and rugby league. A number of reasons can be advanced by way of an explanation, the most obvious and convincing being the relatively homogeneous and autonomous nature of the sport as a sub-field. Until relatively late into the twentieth century, English cricket was dominated by traditional and strongly conservative institutions such as the MCC, county club committees and *Wisdens*, few of whom were enthusiastic about widening their demographic or entering into closer relations with business or the media. Much like rugby in England, Scotland and Australia (but not in Wales, New Zealand or France), cricket was happy to keep its distance from the lower-classes, profit-driven enterprises and media circuses. Guttmann points out that:

> There was little effort to lure the lower classes from their pubs and music halls. Those who administered the game simply renounced the economic principle of profit-maximization that might have led them to seek larger and more socially heterogeneous crowds. As P.F. Warner announced in 1912, 'cricket is not a circus, and it would be far better that it should be driven back to the village green, where it found its origins, than yield a jot to the petulant demands of the spectators'. Displeased sensation-seekers were advised to stay at home, 'and the game will be none the worse for their absence'. (1986: 102)

Another reason that cricket maintained its traditional, conservative and elitist character (in England at least) was the influence exerted by public school-educated journalists and writers such as Warner, Cardus and R.H. Lyttleton, and radio commentators such as Howard Marshall, who in response to Len Hutton scoring a painfully slow triple century against Australia at the Oval, wrote that "While we may reasonably be pleased at England's mastery, I cannot believe that any true lover of cricket will be easy in his mind about the conditions in which it was achieved" (Birley 2003: 258). Cricket journalism and literature have usually stood apart and consciously differentiated themselves from popular journalism, with its emphasis on the hyperbolic, the spectacle, the action-hero narrative and the glorifying of ends rather than means.

Moreover, and unlike baseball, cricketing journalists and spectators never adopted a fetishistic attitude towards, or even a particularly high regard for, statistics. Whereas a baseball box-score provides multiple and unfolding layers of information, a cricket score-card is relatively flat: there are eight columns in a baseball box-score for batters and pitchers, but a score-card usually only has three for the batting side (the name of the batter, how he or she was dismissed and by whom, and the runs scored) and five for the bowlers (name, overs, maidens, wickets, runs). There is additional information such as the order in which a team batted, but there is no accumulative or accretive dimension to the statistics (say with regard to number of centuries scored or bowling average), and nothing about fielding errors. Baseball, which has its own culture of serious journalistic and literary writing, often uses statistics as a departure point – ERA comparisons, the home run record, the perfect or complete game, or hitting a grand slam. The cricket score-card, on the other hand, is often merely an adjunct to a journalistic report which, while not necessarily eschewing the dramatic or the statistical, necessarily reserves a place for the ethical and the stylish.

CONCLUSION

The examples of cricket, baseball and American college football demonstrate how different sports, in tandem with and through the media, developed types or genres of spectatorship with specific dimensions and narratives: cricket with its class-based ethics, aesthetics and nostalgia for the village green; baseball as statistical empire and the game of and from an idealized rural America; and college football as social ritual-as-network and business. All popular sport – and the field of sport itself – partook of and was transformed by this experience. Even cricket, which clearly had a strong antipathy with regard to the commercializing and crass publicizing of the game, was forced to work with the media in order to discipline it; that is, it wanted to produce forms of spectatorship and journalistic texts that mirrored the values and rhythms of the game. And just like every other popular sport, cricket ended up making a spectacle of itself. In our next chapter we will discuss the relation between sport and spectacle, and (related) developments with regard to spectatorship, from the early twentieth century to the present.

7 From Sport to Spectacle

INTRODUCTION

In the previous chapter we looked at how, during the latter part of the nineteenth century, the media promoted sport to a wider demographic, and to a large extent invented the modern notion of sports spectatorship. This promotion of and focus on sport certainly helped boost the media by way of newspaper sales and, as communication technology developed, increased radio and television ratings and advertising revenue. In the process it also completely transformed sport and its logics, practices, meanings and sociocultural functions. Sports such as cricket, soccer, cycling, baseball and American college football simultaneously became spectator-oriented and important sites of national and communal identity (insofar as those identities had an overwhelmingly male inflection), and consequently of greater interest to businesses (as commodities in their own rights, but also as vehicles for advertising) and governments (as a means of improving the health and fitness of populations, integrating and interpolating ethnic communities into nationalist narratives, and promoting nations and ideologies on a world stage).

The most important of these developments, presaged by the advent of radio broadcasts of baseball, college football, soccer and boxing and other popular sports in the 1920s, is what Guy Debord refers to as the society of the spectacle (1983). In his discussion of the relationship between the concept spectacle and Michel Foucault's notions of surveillance and biopower (Foucault 1995), Crary makes the following observation:

> Foucault's opposition of surveillance and spectacle seems to overlook how the effects of the two regimes of power can coincide ... Foucault relentlessly emphasizes the ways in which human subjects become objects of observation, in

the form of institutional control or scientific or behavioural study; but he neglects the new forms by which vision itself became a kind of discipline or mode of work ... nineteenth century optical devices, no less than the panopticon, involved arrangements of bodies in space, regulation of activity, and the deployment of individual bodies, which codified and normalized the observer within rigidly defined systems of visual consumption. They were techniques for the arrangement of attention, for imposing homogeneity, anti-nomadic procedures that fixed and isolated the observer ... The organization of mass culture ... was fully embedded within the same transformations Foucault outlines. (1998: 18)

There are four main inter-related conditions or characteristics of the spectacle outlined here. First, attention is all-important – it must be attracted and maintained. Second, vision is arranged, organized and disposed within various hegemonic visual regimes, the most influential and pervasive of which is that of capitalism. Third, everything is (potentially) reduced to the status of commodity, and there is an emphasis on necessary, repetitive and mobile (visual) consumption. Fourth, the subject-as-spectator relates to the social and the self through the consumption of commodities: this process stands in for, and functions as a simulation of, the social. In other words spectacle is not primarily concerned with looking or content, but rather with the "construction of conditions that individuate, immobilize and separate subjects, even within a world in which mobility and circulation are ubiquitous" (Crary 1998: 74). Crary goes on to suggest that the notion of the spectacle as posited by Debord "probably does not effectively take shape until several decades into the twentieth century" (1998: 18).

SPORT AS SPECTACLE

How and to what extent does the notion of spectacle inform what is happening in and to the field of sport in the late nineteenth and early twentieth centuries? In *Association Football and English Society: 1863–1915* (1980) Tony Mason traces the most significant changes in soccer as a spectator event from the late 1870s, when games were beginning to attract moderately large crowds and incipient attempts were being made to promote and advertise games. Importantly, this was accompanied by the first consistent articulations of codes of behaviour for, and the organization and arrangement of, soccer spectators. Before 1880 this was a very modest enterprise: very few games drew in excess of ten thousand spectators, there was no integration of the event into communication and transport networks, and only limited information was available about match-ups and schedules. As Mason explains, going to the soccer at this time was very much 'of the moment':

How did these crowds come together? In the 1870s, how did they find out that football matches were taking place, and how did they reach the venue? If we look first at how people discovered that football matches were to be played at a particular time and place then obviously those people living close to the ground had something of an advantage. They might see a match in progress, or the players going to the ground. They might be told about it by a player, a watcher, or some other branch of the local grapevine. In the early years of Newton Heath F. C. in the 1880s, matches 'were advertised largely by locally distributed "team sheets" which shopkeepers willingly placed in their windows'. Such local community advertising must have been widespread. By the 1880s posters were common enough. (1980: 144)

This is hardly the pre-condition for spectacle: the crucial issue of attention is absent, and there is no serious attempt at influencing or directing the gaze of spectators. Spectator sport, at least in Britain, was still what we might characterize as a relatively disorganized and open fantasy space: there were levels of identification where spectators more or less self-interpellated (vis-à-vis a team, a player, a style of play or even the sport itself), but this process was, like the decision to go the match, relatively arbitrary and isolated. The relationships and processes that linked play-as-escape (going to and being caught up in the match) to wider social identities, meanings and activities were both nascent and as yet not fully incorporated into communication, transport, economic and socio-cultural networks. To some extent this remained the case until at least after the Second World War, and perhaps until the advent of the technology-driven global networks that developed over the last quarter of the twentieth century. But in the last decade of the nineteenth century organized sport took the first steps towards becoming an organized form of mass, spectator-inflected consumer culture.

In Britain the railway provided relatively cheap and fast services that allowed clubs such as Aston Villa, Sunderland, Sheffield Wednesday, Preston North End and Wolverhampton Wanderers to draw spectators from increasingly wider catchment areas; and thanks to the standardization and widespread dissemination and publicizing of fixture lists fans could read about and plan excursions to games all over the country. The advent of professionalism and national competitions was accompanied by the emergence of high profile teams (Preston North End in the 1880s, Sunderland and Aston Villa in the 1890s, Manchester United and Newcastle United in the new century) which "after the local heroes, were probably the subjects of most of the football conversations in the street or public house, at home or work" (Mason 1980: 216). The players and teams and the competitions they took place in (Football League, FA Cup, Home Championship) were also increasingly textualized and, as a corollary, commoditized in and through the media: newspapers enthusiastically and frequently reported on, analyzed, promoted and informed readers about the game. On game day the papers used the telephone, telegraph and new printing machines to turn out numerous up-to-the-hour editions with details of results, scorers and accounts of play. By the 1890s "few towns of any size in England were without their football special. It was as much a part of the cultural scene as the gas lamp and the fish and chip shop" (Mason 1980: 193).

The idea of playing sport was seen as providing a valuable contribution to the health and moral fibre of the nation; but the same could not be said, initially at least, of sport as a spectator event. The discourses and ethos that emanated from public school culture, and which effectively defined and organized the field of sport well into the twentieth century, elevated the active player as much as it denigrated "the passive onlooker at a spectacle" (Crary 1998: 5). But the arguments and logics that allowed for the non-upper classes to benefit from playing team sports (often through the efforts of and the persuasion exercised by public school educated state school teachers, health professionals and the proponents of muscular Christianity) could and were extended, in a variety of forms, to lower- and middle-class spectatorship. Walking to a game or standing in the open air could be considered healthy exercise – particularly if the alternative was heavy alcohol consumption; and it "provided working men with something to do, even if it was only watching twenty two hirelings kick an inflated piece of leather about" (Mason 1980: 226). This was a considerably less threatening scenario than the alternatives considered by the newspaper proprietor Lord Birkenhead:

> What would the devotees of athletics do if their present amusements were abolished? The policeman, the police magistrate, the social worker, the minister of religion, the public schoolmaster and the University don would each, in the sphere of his own duties, contemplate such a prospect with dismay. Is it to be supposed, for instance, that the seething mass of humanity which streams every Saturday at mid-day out of the factories and workshops of our great towns would ever saunter in peace and contentment through museums and picture galleries, or sit enraptured listening to classical concerts ... The poorer classes in this country have not got the tastes which superior people or a Royal Commission would choose for them, and were cricket and football abolished, it would bring upon the masses nothing but misery, depression, sloth, indiscipline, and disorder". (Mason 1980: 226–7)

MEDIA, SPECTACLE AND COMMUNITY

Sport was also seen as an occasion and space when class differences could be erased and replaced by a sense of community – either at the level of city, county, region or (particularly in time of war) nation. This notion of sport-as-community was accentuated, in Britain and the Empire, Europe and in the United States, by developments in media technology – initially radio and newsreel film, and then somewhat later, television. In Britain the BBC enjoyed a radio monopoly from the 1920s to the mid-1950s, and the imperatives that animated John Reith's version of public service broadcasting – educating the population in and disseminating values and attitudes that were, simultaneously, the core of the nation and the means of imagining it in existence – were addressed in its coverage of sport. Entertainment, hyperbole, populism, hero worship and parochialism were not strongly in evidence: BBC broadcasts were meant to be informative and analytical. Listeners were told what was happening and why, but the relation of commentators to both the events and the audience was one of disinterested interestedness. BBC sporting broadcasts also had a strong elitist inflection: commentators were usually products of, closely aligned with, and promoted the ethos derived from and identifiable with, public school culture. This explains not just the accents and pedagogical bent of the commentators, but also which sports were privileged as embodying the best aspects of Englishness, and those that were not. Cricket and rugby received levels of coverage disproportionate to their popular appeal; soccer was an institution – albeit a popular one – and couldn't be ignored; but rugby league, a profes-sionalized version of rugby union that was confined to the north of England:

> was not considered to be a sport whose main event (the cup final) should be regarded as a 'must'. Rather, like wrestling and cycling, it was seen as being unsuitable for radio, and ... was 'treated very cautiously as a socially inferior local sport'. (Hill 2002: 49)

In the United States radio simply picked up, accentuated and extended the media–sports nexus that had developed in the last decade of the nineteenth century. By the 1920s:

> Babe Ruth's prodigious exploits on the baseball diamond, the college football craze, the rise of professional golf and tennis, and a host of other athletic activities captured the nation's attention. Anyone in the United States, through newspaper accounts and nationwide radio broadcasts, could participate in the sports craze. Spectatorship marked one of the new sets of behaviours which knitted the nation together into a mass society. (Dyreson 1995: 208)

Radio broadcasts of sport initially had much the same function as that of the newspaper coverage of college football games and baseball at the turn of the century – they were seen as a way to increase both the sale of radios and the size of audiences, and eventually to attract more sponsorship and advertising revenue. The strategy worked: the Jack Dempsey–Georges Carpentier heavyweight fight of 1921, for instance, was broadcast "into movie theatres and assorted halls from Maine to Miami ... and attracted some 300,000 paying listeners" (Mandell 1984: 220); and by the end of the decade "there were more than ten million radios in the nation" (Mandell 1984: 220). The surge in audiences and the ownership of sets was matched by the increase in stations and networks: in the United States radio "was subject only to technical regulation. Radio time was offered to the free market" (Mandell 1984: 221). The development of mechanisms for determining audience sizes in the 1930s led to a tighter competition for advertising revenue, which increased radio's dependence not just on blockbuster events, but also on regular sports broadcasts such as weekly fight nights and daily baseball games.

Radio was even more effective than newspapers in developing the culture of spectatorship and the transformation of sport into spectacle, and in helping to facilitate its integration into the networks and logics of mass consumer culture, for four main reasons. First and foremost, radio coverage of sport was more likely to gain and hold a person's attention because the event was happening and unfolding as they listened; in other words, the potential for tension and drama in a boxing match or a baseball game – a flurry of punches could send one fighter to the canvas, one hit could change the course of the game – not only ensured that the audience stayed on, but it also made them attentive to the broadcast. This relationship was accentuated by broadcasters: they used hyperbole to inflate the significance of what was happening, and kept listeners on tenterhooks by narrating the action in such a way that the game or match always seemed to be at a crucial point. Even someone passing by who would have no particular interest in a boxing match, say, and who would be unlikely to read about it afterwards, could be caught up in the excitement of the moment. Second, radio offered more of an opportunity for the performance of communal identity than was the case with newspapers: a family or group of friends, or even a group of strangers at a bar, could sit in the same space 'listening together'. Third, radio broadcasts continuously reminded listeners that they were part of a wider community-as-audience linked by a set of shared interests, pleasures and values: radio literally addressed, and in the process sought to interpellate, the one and/as the many, with specific references ('you') being mixed in with the general ('folks'), the personal ('my friends in') and the geographical (towns and states). Fourth, links could be made between the events, activities, game, players and the ethos or virtues of sport, on the one hand, and sponsors and advertisers, on the other, in a manner (by timing such a reference to an accomplishment in the game) and with a frequency that surpassed similar practices in the print media.

The same arguments could be made regarding television coverage of sport in Britain and the United States, but in the period prior to the Second World War its impact on sport was relatively minor. In Britain it was "a frivolous gimmick" (Boyle and Haynes 2000: 39), extremely limited in range and audience and technically primitive:

> The sheer bulkiness of the technology required to transmit for sport, specifically the mass of cable involved, severely restricted the mobility of the equipment. The problem of economically marshalling the technology needed on location took many years to resolve. (Boyle and Haynes 2002: 41)

In the United States coverage was considerably greater, but nowhere near as pervasive as was the case with radio – in 1950 "less than 10% of all American homes had television sets" (Baker 1982: 311). The sport that benefited most from television at this time was boxing, which because of the limited physical space of the contest presented fewer technical problems than stadium sports such as baseball, and was ideally "suited to the screen" (Baker 1982: 311). After the Second World War television quickly moved to telecast college football, baseball, basketball and professional American football, and all of these sports benefited as they attracted attracted wider demographics and greater sponsorship and advertising revenue.

The field of sport – particularly in the United States – was increasingly being inflected by the logics and imperatives of the media, but full integration into Debord's 'society of the spectacle' (1983), which is predicated on a configuration of capitalist expansion and technological innovation, was delayed until after the 1960s. Conditions were favourable during the 1890s, but as Karl Polanyi points out the beginning of the twentieth century witnessed both the gradual decline and collapse of the self-regulating market, which was the "key to the institutional system of the nineteenth century" (1957: 3), and concomitantly the 'return of the social', a development accentuated by events such as the First World War and the Great Depression. This manifested itself in a variety of ways, including the promulgation of tariffs restricting access to home markets, the erection of barriers to the movement of migrants-as-labour, patriotic and jingoistic politics, and eventually war. In Britain and across the Empire the strong suspicion of spectatorship, formerly alleviated by the anti-revolutionary logics of Lord Birkenhead, reappeared during the Boer War and the First World War. The ascent of militarism meant that sport itself become slightly suspect. In 1902 *The Times* "published Kipling's famous panegyric on a decadent nation 'The Islanders'" where he "criticised a country that spent so much time and energy on sport and yet refused to master the arts of warfare" (Mason 1980: 239); and contrasts were frequently drawn between the serious, industrious and efficient Germans and the frivolous sports playing and watching British. Nonetheless the most concerted, organized and widely networked example of sport-as-spectacle in the first half of the twentieth century took place in Germany: the Berlin Olympics of 1936 made use of public relations techniques and advanced communication/media technologies for propagandist rather than commercial purposes; and it served as a kind of unacknowledged template for sport in the post-World War Two communist world, most notably the Soviet Union.

SPECTACLE AND THE SOVIET UNION

The development of sport-as-spectacle in the Soviet Union had its own particular vicissitudes that both overlapped with, and distinguished it from, what was happening in Britain, Europe and the United States. In the period after the revolution gymnastics and drilling took precedence over competitive sport, which was viewed with suspicion because of its association with 'bourgeois' spectatorship, parochialism and professionalism. When the Soviet Union did take up sport it initially had a strong participatory inflection, and government policy followed the late-nineteenth British and American examples of using it as a means of improving health and fitness, combating alcoholism, and providing military-style training and discipline. During the 1930s the emphasis changed: national leagues were established in popular sports such as soccer and ice hockey, which were dominated by the newly formed sports societies (bearing what were to become famous generic names of Torpedo, Spartak, Dinamo and Lokomotiv) linked to workplace sectors such as the military, the railway workers, the automobile industry and the police. These competitions and clubs "created new interest and mass appeal, especially in the most popular male team-game, soccer, and drew many thousands of spectators to view important matches" (Riordan 1978a: 24).

What was happening with sport in the Soviet Union (national competitions, the emergence of clubs which were the focus of larger communal identities, an increase in specialization and some level of professionalism, incipient spectatorship) to some extent mirrored the contexts and developments that had characterized Britain in the last quarter of the nineteenth century. Soviet policy, which had effectively utilized sport as a means for implementing techniques of bio-power within the frame of the reason of state, shifted its emphasis onto the socio-cultural (most particularly, recreational and spectatorial) functions of sport:

> The Soviet society of the 1930s differed from that of the preceding period in seeing the flourishing of all manner of competitive sports … with mass spectator

appeal and the official encouragement of leagues, stadiums, cups, championships, popularity-polls, cults of sporting heroes – all the appendages of a sub-
system designed to provide general recreation for the fast-growing urban
populace ... Millions of people, uprooted from centuries-old traditions, were
pitched into new and strange environments ... Since urban living conditions
were spartan and deteriorating, sport served many townsmen as an escape from
the drudgery of their domestic and work environments. The many sports-
parades and pageants which constituted a background to the sports contests of
the 1930s were intended, too, to create and reinforce a 'togetherness', to evoke
feelings of patriotism, and to demonstrate to people (abroad as well as at home)
how happy and carefree life was under socialism in the USSR ... It is significant
that sports rallies often accompanied major political events or festivals ... In
this way, sport became a means of linking members of the public with politics,
the Party and, of course, Stalin. (Riordan 1978a: 25–7)

Media coverage of sport had two main functions. First, during the
"'besieged fortress' atmosphere of the 1930s", which was a product of both
the rise of Fascism and the "deliberate playing up of the danger from without" (Riordan 1978a: 27), the media had to impress upon the population
that the good citizen was one who was not only willing, but also physically
capable, of defending the country – and sport was a principal means by which
this could be achieved. Second and concomitantly, the scenes and spaces of
sport (the stadium, the crowd, the game) had to be represented and experienced as the state manifested in all its fullness. In other words what newspapers, radio journalists and newsreel directors had to do was to convince
their audiences (or at least to get them to act as if they were convinced) that
the crowd of which they were a part, the game being played before them,
and the interaction between the two were examples of and organically
linked to the (utopian) idea made flesh that was the Soviet Union. The way
of achieving this was through the representation of the exemplary (but
simultaneously typical) socialist sporting body, either within or via the mediation of official texts (public art, film, radio, newspaper articles). When
spectators saw photographs of, read articles about, or watched sport they
were disposed to see and experience the text in terms of how, under Stalinist
socialism, the ordinary person had become heroic and was motivated to
perform extraordinary deeds.

When Soviet sport (and sport in the other eastern bloc nations) took to
the international stage, it became an important means for demonstrating "to
the world the superiority of the 'socialist' system of government" (Mandell
1984: 249). By the late 1940s sport had taken on a role – not just in the
Soviet Union, but also in Bulgaria, Czechoslovakia, Hungary, Poland and
most particularly the German Democratic Republic – as one of the key cultural weapons of the Cold War. This involved systematically encouraging
and identifying talent, developing more scientific regimes of training, and

the de facto adoption of full professionalism. From the end of the Second World War to the collapse of the Soviet Union the field of sport in the socialist/communist world became the focus of a centralized concentration and amalgamation – a unparalleled symbiosis – of the principles of the reason of state (populations were viewed, appropriated and trained as potential sporting resources) and spectacle (the mass media ensured that both the stadiums that hosted national and international competitions, as well as the local school sports field and swimming pool, became synonymous with socialist identity), as this description of the organization of sport in the GDR makes clear:

> In August 1948 the ... German Sports Committee ... was announced ... the DSA had a virtual monopoly-position in regard to sport ... It was put in charge of all educational institutions concerned with sport, of all sports activities in schools and universities, and was responsible for all research work in this field. Further, it played an important role in the treatment of sport in the mass media ... Even at this time attempts were made to make sport in the GDR something of a mass activity ... (a) March 1951 Resolution claimed that some 750,000 members were in the 'Democratic Sports Movement'. This was in a country which at that time had a population of some 18.3 million ... The ... Resolution announced the setting up of special boarding schools for children of fourteen and over who had a special talent for sport ... The Resolution also called for compulsory sport in all trade-union and factory-based schools. (Childs 1978: 76–7)

SPORT AND INTERNATIONAL POLITICS

The integration of the communist world into the wider field of sport seemed an unlikely possibility in the late 1940s: the Soviets and their allies were committed to a policy of isolationism, and concentrated instead on big internal and overtly propagandist spectacles such as the four-yearly Spartakiads, or sports festivals. However, as the Cold War intensified the Soviets moved to a policy of achieving 'world supremacy' (Riordan 1977: 165), which necessitated that they join and compete in prestigious events such as the soccer World Cup and the Olympics. The Olympic movement was ambivalent about the question of eastern bloc membership: it welcomed the increased competition and the boost in standards that Soviet participation would provide, but it was concerned about the possibility of the Games being overtly politicized, IOC representatives not acting and voting independently, and the amateur status of Soviet athletes.

The IOC prided itself on being the keeper of the flame of the true spirit of sport and its attendant ethics and virtues, and was determined to avoid any overt politicizing of the games. There was also concern about the apparent 'professional' status of Soviet athletes. The Olympic movement had been relatively inconsistent in taking action against breaches of amateurism: now and then a high profile athlete who had flagrantly breached the rules (such as Jim Thorpe in 1912 and Paavo Nurmi in 1932) was made an example of, but, much like the Welsh Rugby Union and the International Lawn Tennis Association, the IOC operated under double standards. Even prior to the 1930s many of the best athletes were supported to the extent that their 'real jobs' in the military or police force were convenient fictions – although as Guttmann points out apropos of equestrian riders in the immediate post-Second World War period "By Alice-in-Wonderland definition, officers who spent their lives in the saddle were amateurs but an ordinary soldier was a professional" (1992: 85). Alternatively they were provided with university scholarships, which effectively allowed them to train and prepare as more or less full-time professionals (that fount of professional amateurism, the American college system, was particularly egregious in this regard). Olympic rules required that:

> all athletes be certified as amateurs by their national Olympic committees, but as (then IOC president) Edstrom confided to Brundage in a letter ... 'We must face the fact that many of them [Soviet athletes] are professional'. Since Pravda routinely announced the cash prizes and awards given to successful Soviet athletes, it was not exactly a secret that these men and women were indeed 'state amateurs'. As such, they were unquestionably ineligible to compete in the Olympics. (Guttmann 1992: 88)

The problems didn't end there: Olympic rules also stipulated that "every national Olympic committee must be independent of the government ... Neither Edstrom nor Brundage had any illusions about the political independence of the Soviet National Olympic Committee" (Guttmann 1992: 88). In the end the lure of a greatly enhanced and more competitive Olympic Games overcame the collective misgivings of the IOC which, in the best Stalinist tradition, simply 'disappeared' the problems: in Guttmann's words, "the solution was for the IOC collectively to close its eyes and pretend that the Russian athletes were amateurs and that the national Olympic committee never gave a thought to the people in the Kremlin" (1992: 88).

It's not an exaggeration to talk about the transformation of the Olympic Games, the IOC and more generally the field of sport after the communist nations were admitted to the Olympic movement (the Soviets, Hungarians and the Czechs competed in the summer Games in Helsinki in 1952, the GDR in Melbourne in 1956 (Riordan 1977). Some signs of these changes were at the level of the blatant intrusion of the political: examples include Stalin's refusal to allow the Olympic torch to travel across the USSR in

1952; the saga of the struggle between Taiwan and the People's Republic as to who represented China; and the defection of a large percentage of the Hungarian team at, and the partial boycott (by Egypt, Iraq and Lebanon) of, the Melbourne games as a result of political and military intervention in Hungary and Egypt, respectively. But the main sporting refraction of the wider socio-political tensions of the Cold War was played out, in both the Western and the Soviet mass media, through the policy of using sport as (Cold) war by other means.

The European communist nations lobbied for changes to the IOC relationship between the IOC and national Olympic committees, the expansion of IOC membership, financial arrangements, and the geographical distribution of membership (Guttmann 1992: 90). They succeeded in introducing a level of democratization into what was an unashamedly autocratic and elitist organization, and presaged even more significant changes such as the 'rebellion' of the NOCs and international federations (which eventually led to the overthrow of Brundage as president) and the suspension and then expulsion of South Africa and Rhodesia. The IOC, and the field of sport in general, tended to shy away from overt politics, but the Soviets established a direct and more or less necessary articulation between sporting success and political and ideological value. Once this logic was in place it was difficult for any group identity (national, regional, political or ethnic) to ignore or refuse it, and sport became a substitute site for the playing out of ideological, national and ethnic rivalries. The Hungarian triumph in the gold medal water polo game at the 1956 Melbourne Olympics passed into sporting mythology, in Australia and throughout the west, as an example of and a metaphor for a brave and oppressed people resisting Soviet tyranny; at the 1968 Olympics in Mexico George Foreman's flag-waving after his triumph over his Soviet opponent carried considerable symbolic weight, as did the victories of the Czech gymnast Vera Caslavska over competitors from eastern bloc countries that had invaded her country; and three Afro-Americans – the sprinters Lee Evans, Tommy Smith and John Carlos – protested against American racism, exemplified by the assassination of Martin Luther King and the violence directed against civil rights protests in the southern states of America. The Soviet victory over the United States in basketball in Munich in 1972, and the United States defeat of the Soviets in ice hockey at the Lake Placid winter games of 1980, were particularly celebrated and mythologized because of the underdog status of the winners and the traditionally close association between the particular sport and the losers.

As the political function of sport became more accentuated, so did the likelihood of direct state intervention in the field of sport. Germany had only been allowed to keep the 1936 Olympics because Hitler had promised to allow the German sports officials not just his support but also, crucially, a free hand in the selection of the team. This meant that (theoretically) Jewish and other non-Aryan athletes were eligible for selection. In practice this didn't happen (Jews were expelled from athletic organizations and clubs, which effectively deprived them of the means of competing and making a case for selection), but it demonstrated how, at a discursive level, the state needed to (perform) respect for the autonomy of sport. By the 1960s this was no longer the case: in 1968 the exclusion of Basil D'Oliveira from a MCC team to tour South Africa eventually led to that country being excluded from authorized international cricket and rugby competitions; on a more dramatic level, Israeli athletes were taken hostage and murdered at the Munich games in 1972 in an attempt to secure the release of members of the Baader-Meinhoff group and Palestinian prisoners held in Israel (Guttmann 1992). Political issues continued to be played out at the Games between 1976 and 1984: prior to the Montreal Games the Canadian government refused visas to the Taiwanese team, and many African nations stayed away because of New Zealand's rugby contacts with South Africa; and the Moscow Games were boycotted by the USA and its allies, some Islamic nations and the People's Republic of China, because of the USSR's intervention in Afghanistan.

The background to the boycott of the Moscow Olympics provided a particularly good example of the extent to which international sport had become subjected to logics, strategies and imperatives emanating from the field of politics:

> In January 1980, President Jimmy Carter of the USA warned the Soviet government that its failure to withdraw troops from Afghanistan might lead to an American boycott of the Olympics; when the 20 February deadline was missed, the United States Olympic Committee, under pressure from the government, voted in favour of a boycott. In the UK, the new Conservative government showed its support for the Americans by backing the boycott: Prime Minister Margaret Thatcher later claimed that 'the most effective thing we could do [to take action against the USSR] would be to prevent their using the forthcoming Moscow Olympics for propaganda purposes'. However ... the BOA refused to co-operate with this line ... Its line was that it was being used as a high profile pawn. The BOA refused to be used in isolation from other Anglo-Soviet contacts in trade and diplomacy that were not being threatened because sport was so public and emotive. (Polley 1998: 32)

In the end the British team went to Moscow, but only after resisting "government ... bullying tactics, including the refusal of leave to civil servants competing" (Polley 1998: 33). The games were treated as a propaganda opportunity, and by and large the media facilitated this effect. In the opening ceremony sixteen teams, including that from Britain, "marched behind the Olympic rings or the ensign of their national Olympic committee" as a form of protest against what was happening in Afghanistan, but "none of these banners were shown on Soviet television" (Guttmann 1992: 155). Tass, Pravda and other news outlets condemned the absence of the sixty odd nations as a violation of the autonomy of sport, and rationalized it as an attempt by the Americans and their cronies to avoid athletic humiliation.

At Los Angeles in 1984 the eastern bloc boycott enabled the Americans to dominate, to the unfettered delight of local spectators and the ABC television network, which did its best to ignore any non-American victories – with the notable exception of those involving the Romanians, whose appearance in defiance of the Soviets was celebrated as a triumph of sport over politics. If the Moscow Games had showcased and performed the virtues of communism, Los Angeles functioned as a media-driven spectacle of sport saturated in patriotic American can-do capitalism:

> Olympic organizer Peter Ueberroth raised half a billion dollars by selling advertising rights to more than thirty companies, including refuse companies that bid for the right to pick up Olympic garbage. By making commercial sponsorship a significant revenue stream, the first-ever privately financed games paid for themselves, turning a profit of $215 million. Like his fellow entrepreneurs Lee Iacocca, Donald Trump, and Ted Turner, Ueberroth was widely celebrated as the living embodiment of a new ethos of capitalist success, an example of what could happen when governments got out of the way and let markets operate freely. *Time* magazine named Ueberroth the 'Man of the Year' for devising a privatized model to finance the Olympics that transformed them into a money-making spectacle. (Jay 2004: 181–2)

The 1984 event was extravagantly over-the-top and commercialized, but it became the template for future Games, as well as exemplifying what sport had become and presaging where it was going. The amount of money that came in from advertising, sponsorship and television rights (ABC paid US$225 million, an increase of 250% on Moscow) was a sign of an increasing commercialization of sporting events and practices.

CONCLUSION

These changes inflected or transformed most practices and dispositions within the field of sport. In the next two decades athletes would sometimes refrain from attempting to break world records if it was not financially advantageous; a century of sporting rivalries and traditions in British soccer became irrelevant, as teams such as Manchester United and Chelsea sought to leave the Premier League for a private and elitist European competition and fielded reserve sides in FA Cup matches, which they treated as a distraction; the strongly amateur and participatory sport of rugby would, after one hundred and fifty years, embrace open professionalism; and soccer clubs would sign players not so much because of their sporting ability or to fill team needs, but rather in terms of their potential for generating advertising and sponsorship revenue (as Real Madrid did with David Beckham). Cricket, the bastion of establishment sport, had by this time already succumbed to Kerry Packer's version of bread and circuses, and was well on the way to reinventing and redefining itself as a television-friendly event (limited overs games were now a serious threat to, rather than a flippant diversion from, test matches) with the ability and willingness to appeal to a wider demographic. In our next chapter we look at how these processes have been played out up to and including the early years of the twenty-first century.

8 Contemporary Sport

INTRODUCTION

In previous chapters we've followed the field of sport from its beginnings in English public schools to its transformation into a global media spectacle. This chapter takes up the story of sport in what we can call its contemporary phase (over the last forty years or so), in which time the relatively incipient and equivocal relationship that the field developed with media, capitalism and government has become a symbiosis. We'll focus on the relationship between the set of authorized discourses and narratives that characterize the field and the new social, cultural, political, technological and economic contexts in which they operate. It may "go without saying" (Bourdieu 1991a: 366), but it still needs to be said that:

> the popularization of sport, down from the elite schools (where its place is now contested by the 'intellectual' pursuits imposed by the demands of intensified social competition) to the mass sporting associations, is necessarily accompanied by a change in the functions which the sportsmen and their organizers assign to this practice, and also by a transformation of the very logic of sporting practices which correspond to the transformation of the expectations and demands of the public in correlation with the increasing autonomy of the spectacle vis-à-vis past or present practice. The exaltation of 'manliness' and the cult of 'team spirit' that are associated with playing rugby – not to mention the aristocratic ideal of 'fair play' – have a very different meaning and function for bourgeois or aristocratic adolescents in English public schools and for the sons of peasants or shopkeepers in south-west France. (366)

Sport has tended to represent itself as sequestered and utopian: both a world within itself and a kind of exemplar of what the wider world should be like – hence those Olympic posters that promote the games as a vehicle for global harmony, tolerance and understanding. But from the beginning the claims it made about its autonomy and disinterestedness placed it firmly within the world – one that was upper class, elitist, patriarchal, white and English. The field continues to refer back to its public school origins, but in its current manifestation it would have been unimaginable or anathema to the English patrician classes of the 1860s.

SPORT AND TELEVISION

We pointed out that prior to the Second World War television had a minimal impact on the field of sport. Initially radio dominated sports coverage in both the USA and the UK, but this changed quickly in the United States: television attracted large audiences with its telecasts of boxing and college football in the 1940s and 1950s, and generally replaced radio to the extent that while the latter had been an "essential part of daily life" in America in the 1930s, by the end of the 1940s "the average American listened to the radio for only twenty four minutes a day" (Guttmann 1986: 134). In Britain the changeover was more gradual due to the well-established status and influence of BBC radio and the relatively slow development of a national transmitter system, but whereas in "early 1950s less than 5% of households" possessed television sets, by the 1970s "this was the proportion of those that did not" (Hill 2002: 103).

This did not at first translate, however, into wide and consistent live television coverage of mass spectator sport: there was a suspicion on the part of many sports administrators that such a move would mean lower attendances. This had been the case in the USA with boxing telecasts, which led to falls in attendances at Madison Square Garden of up to 80% in the 1940s (Guttmann 1986: 135), and while there had been a remarkable post-war (and pre-television) increase in attendances at English soccer, cricket and rugby league matches, by the 1960s:

> The number of paying spectators was falling across the board, a trend that continued in the 1970s and beyond … For 1969–70, for example, Football League attendances fell to 29.6 million, a drop of 28 per cent in twenty one seasons, with the low point coming in 1984–5 when only 17.8 million attended, down 56 per cent from the post-war boom. In county cricket, a decline was evident by the early 1960s with the 'nadir' reached in 1966 when '513,578 individuals went through the county turnstiles', a mere 22 per cent of the crowds in 1947. The rugby league Challenge Cup Final continued to draw large crowds … but after the record crowd at Odsal for the 1954 replay, the fixture … failed to fill Wembley on thirty occasions. A more noticeable decline was evident in the league fixtures: by 1968–9, attendances had fallen to 2.7 million, a drop of 60 per cent over twenty one seasons … This was a time of the game's catastrophic

decline as a spectator sport ... (and) examples can be multiplied across the other spectator sports. (Polley 1998: 71)

Martin Polley identifies a number of reasons for this trend, including increase in available leisure activities, a switch to individual sports participation, the primitive state of stadium facilities and hooliganism and crowd disorders; but clearly one of the most significant factors was "the increasing amount of television sport which allowed potential spectators to sample a greater variety of events than they could ever see live without having to pay ... or leave their own homes" (1998: 72). The other side of the decline in live attendances from the 1960s onward was a concomitant development of television interest in established sports such as golf, tennis, athletics, horseracing and boxing, relatively minor sports such as snooker and darts, overseas sports (the NFL, Australian rules, Sumo wrestling) and even non-sports ('professional wrestling', poker). Soccer, because of its mass spectator appeal, had the most to lose from the televising of sport, but it was also the biggest prize for and target of the BBC, ITV and later on Rupert Murdoch's satellite broadcaster BSkyB. Highlights of games were first shown in 1960s on 'Match of the Day', but the FA resisted live coverage until the early 1980s. The competition for the rights to broadcast games had been played out, during the 1970s and 1980s, between the terrestrial BBC and ITV networks, but in 1992 BSkyB paid over 300 million pounds for a five-year deal involving live coverage, then upped this to 670 million pounds for four years in 1997, and over a million pounds for exclusive live rights until 2007. The growing importance of television income has been repeated in and was particularly pronounced with regard to the biggest national (Wimbledon, the FA Cup final, the Oxford–Cambridge boat race, rugby internationals) and international (Olympics, soccer World Cup, European Cup/Champions League, Tour de France) competitions and events, to the extent that with Wimbledon, for example, television rights provide three times the revenue derived from ticket sales (Horne *et al.* 1999: 279).

Once this culture of and audience for television sport developed, it fed back into and influenced the field in a number of ways. At a very basic level, television more or less picked up and tied itself to certain sports and events and ignored others. Soccer, the Five/Six Nations, the British Open golf and Wimbledon already had mass audiences and high media profiles. In such cases, capital simply attracted capital: demographics widened; sponsorship, advertising and broadcast rights revenue poured in; and salaries and prize-money soared. The revenue that soccer, rugby, baseball, NFL, NBA, ice hockey, golf and tennis derive from television rights and sponsorship (gate takings are becoming less significant) has driven up salaries and earnings to levels unimaginable a decade earlier. Some professional leagues have introduced schemes (such as the salary cap and the draft system of the NFL, NHL and the NBA in the USA) that are meant to curb costs and ensure a relatively even distribution of talent. But, in unregulated leagues such as the MLB, teams like Montreal, Kansas City, Tampa Bay, Pittsburgh, Cleveland and Milwaukee are forced to trade their best players for cheaper prospects in order to stay afloat (in the case of Montreal, the club/franchise simply moved to Washington). Brand names, sponsorship and advertising, population and the size of the television market are now far more significant factors in a team's viability than sporting prowess or tradition: in the NHL there are teams in non-traditional hockey areas such as Atlanta, Florida, Nashville, Tampa Bay, Carolina, Anaheim, Los Angeles, San Jose and Dallas, but not in Quebec City, where a disproportionately high percentage of professional players were born and raised. In Britain it is likely that within a decade over a hundred years of institutionalized soccer competitions and rivalries (the English and Scottish championships and the FA Cup, and derby games such as Manchester United–Manchester City and Liverpool–Everton) will be made redundant or downgraded as the bigger and more affluent clubs (the top English sides plus Celtic and Rangers) move to some form of a permanent British or European league.

Some low-profile sports benefited from these changes, primarily because they were seen as 'television friendly'. In snooker and darts the cameras could follow the action easily while also focusing intimately on the face and expressions of the players and the reactions of the crowd, allowing commentators to 'build up' every shot or throw, which was perfect for creating and showing tension, suspense, drama and passion and promoting larger-than-life or eccentric characters. Sports such as squash, table tennis, badminton, sailing and athletic field events, on the other hand, suffered precisely because they weren't television-friendly. Squash, for instance, was both architecturally unsuitable (players could come between the ball and cameras placed behind or above the action), as well as being simply too fast for spectators to follow or for commentators to do much more than 'talk across' the action. Most tellingly, a great deal of time could be expended in a rally where the players hit the ball up and down the wall waiting for a mistake, and if the point went against the server then (as far as television was concerned) 'nothing had happened' – and it had taken a long time to not happen. Contrast this with an NFL game, where each play can be anticipated, explained and analyzed (by the main commentators, special comments person, sideline reporters, etc.) and broken down into multi-angled slow motion 'slices', and where the frequency of time outs and changes of possession allows for the insertion of numerous commercial breaks. Faced with declining participation numbers and revenue, squash officials did everything to revamp the game for television, including introducing fluorescent balls and transparent walls and changing the scoring system, but nothing really worked: most squash events are in more or less the same position as FIFA in 1954, which gave away the television rights to the tournament in Switzerland "and considered itself lucky to get the publicity" (Guttmann 1986: 135).

There are other effects and consequences of the televising of sport. First, let's consider the issues of space and architecture and their relation to sporting events and crowds. Contemporary stadia are designed and built not just with the game or even the attending spectators in mind (although they must have their own easily visible television screen for instant replays, shots of themselves in the crowd, etc.), but also to cater for the needs of sponsors, advertising and television cameras, and to encourage consumerism and consumption. In short, the shape and contents of stadia (a mixture of functionality and consumerist aesthetics) mirrors both the heterogeneous nature of the field of sport itself, and what we can recognize as the logics and imperatives of spectacle:

> There are few construction processes as those involved in the building of modern stadiums. From space and seats and washrooms for tens of thousands of people, to retractable roofs, to 50 × 80 ft television screens suspended hundreds of feet in the air ... Postmodern stadiums are massive in size, even though their carrying capacity is not increased proportionately ... They are ... ambiguous in the sense that they merge their functions as sports facilities with provisions for banqueting, accommodation (hotels), rented offices, museums and merchandizing. The former mono-functional soccer stadium has given way to a multi-functional business facility ... the interior of the stadium is constructed in such a way that spectator 'sight lines' are unimpeded ... each individual should have a clear, direct view of the action ... Stadiums, as important pieces of architecture, are constructed to be visually consumed ... Totally encircled and domed stadiums ... serve to divorce the stadium experience from the reality of the world around it. This increasing territorialization and commodification turns public space into private space and offers a more particularlized and individualized means of visual consumption ... seeing thousands of other people gathered together in the same place at the same time to partake in a common experience gives one a sense of extended evaluation. One feels something when looking at a crowd of which one is a part. The crowd 'looks at' its self and 'reacts to' its self, which creates an ever-changing experience of its self. (Gaffney and Bale 2004: 27–8)

Perhaps the most significant aspect of this description is the reference to what Baudrillard (1983) would call the simulation of group identity and its packaging as a commodity. The crowd is constantly made aware that it is a crowd, and is prodded (through music, directions from the ground announcer, the antics of the mascot) into performing in line with this genre and its responsibilities and characteristics – it's required to be noisy, involved, interactive, colourful, tense, demonstrative and passionate. In fact the responsibilities of the crowd start before they enter the stadium: colourful and eccentric hats, masks, clothes and scarves should be in evidence; faces painted; signs, flags and posters (preferably making some reference to the relevant television network covering the game) waved; and group chants and routines worked out and practised. On the way to the ground the crowd starts to take shape: it is usually carefully streamed; vendors, hawkers, programme sellers and samplers equip people with flags, rosettes, confectioneries and copies of team line-ups strategically encircled by advertisements; and the first chants, songs, bugle calls, challenges or banter churn out and up the atmosphere. Once inside the stadium everything is done to 'warm the crowd up', with the same purpose as players going through their stretching and skills routines: the ground announcer reminds everyone just how important the game is, what's at stake, and how valuable crowd support is to the team; and the television screen intersperses ads for products and upcoming games with stirring, larger than life scenes of players in action, brawls, controversies and past victories.

Once the game starts it is textualized and disseminated worldwide (on local television screens, satellite networks, packaged highlights down-loaded on digital phones, website reports and up-to-the-minute statistics, as newspaper and magazine articles) and integrated into chrono-logical and spatial rhythms and networks that extend way beyond the here-and-now – and certainly beyond the field of sport. The choice of stadium and the date of play may have been influenced by the proximity of other competing events and/or traffic and transport regimes; the starting time itself may be determined by the desire to ensure that there is a steady stream of games commencing as others finish, and/or to attract tele-vision audiences in other time zones within the country or on the other side of the world; or it may have been scheduled so as to attract and maintain the attention of an audience which can then be passed on to the next televi-sion time-slot and regime of programming, or simply to maximize advertising revenue. If the event is important (a Tri-Nations rugby international, a soccer World Cup match) the best seats in the house will not necessarily be made available to ordinary spectators: premium space will be reserved for corporate boxes which can be used to entertain clients, and other tickets might be distributed to companies who will sell them as part of tourism packages. This exclusivity functions as capital, further enhancing the occa-sion and helping to attract a wider television audience. Giant screens can be set up in public places or clubs, and those crowds and their performances are then integrated into the television and digital network of texts. On the other hand, if the game is having trouble attracting a live crowd, thousands of tickets might be distributed at schools and in shopping centres, simply to provide the semblance of atmosphere and occasion.

This transformation of the sites of spectator sport by the logics and imperatives of television and/as business has had another consequence: as with newspapers in the 1890s and 1900s, television (and by extension the public relations and marketing industries) has taken on the task of widening the sports demographic, and more specifically of promoting sport to groups who know little or nothing of the field, and have cared even less. To some extent this involves selling sports to lucrative non-traditional markets, such as popularizing men's soccer in the United States, rugby in Japan, the NFL in Europe, tennis and golf in China; and attracting women to sports like rugby and soccer. The main BBC sports website, for instance, mixes its up-to-the-minute scores, general sports news and opinion pieces with what can best be termed promotional 'beginners tutorials' on sports skills that usually feature 'of the moment' performers and stars (England cricket players after the 2005 Ashes series, etc.) represented in a style, and at a level, that could only appeal to the non-cognoscenti ('find out how Andy Flintoff gets his reverse swing', 'learn to take a penalty like Thierry Henry'). Basically this is promotion disguised as pedagogy, much as was the case with newspapers at the beginning of the last century.

Jean Baudrillard suggests that one of the defining characteristics of contemporary society is that we live at the pace of objects: "Today it is we who watch them as they are born, grow to maturity and die, whereas in all previous civilizations it was timeless objects, instruments or monuments which outlived the generation of human beings" (Baudrillard 2003: 25). Much the same can be said about sports, teams and competitions. For most of the twentieth century in the southeast of Australia, for instance, a large proportion of the working-class male population grew up with an allegiance to the local rugby league side, which pre-dated (and which they presumed would survive) them. Rugby league provided a culture of continuity and familiarity, involving colours, nicknames, stories, achievements, styles of play, famous players and incidents, rivalries, stadiums and transport grids that linked the area of competition. The movement of players between clubs was relatively infrequent and frowned upon (although not unknown), largely because it called into question their loyalty and integrity. It was easy for fans to identify with players not only because they tended to play for the one team, but also because they were sometimes from the same area (for a time a player was only eligible to play for a side if he lived in that suburb), usually of the same class and educational background, and had a similar bodily shape and hexis.

That culture declined in the 1960s, when live television coverage, and the media exposure and revenue it provided, started to influence salary levels, fixtures and scheduling, and player movements and rules. Like American football at the beginning of the nineteenth century, rugby league was a relatively static game in which one team could easily dominate possession if good enough: accordingly during the 1960s and 1970s the rules were changed to encourage a more open, high scoring and competitive (and television-friendly) contest, with extra points for tries, and limitations placed on how long a side could hold the ball. The traditional game and its culture passed away completely in the 1990s, when the media proprietor Rupert Murdoch organized and financed a rival competition – dubbed 'Superleague' – which was tied to his Sky satellite sports network. After a season the two competitions merged, but Murdoch's television interests, along with those of the Kerry Packer owned and terrestrial Channel Nine network, effectively controlled rugby league from that point on. During and after the struggle for ownership of what had been at one stage a quintessential working-class sport, teams that had been members of the league for most of the century were jettisoned or forced to amalgamate, and completely new sides formed from scratch, sometimes in traditional league areas (working-class Newcastle) and sometime in areas that had never supported the game (Adelaide and Melbourne, where Australian rules dominate). The Adelaide and Melbourne sides attracted paltry crowds, but that wasn't the point: their complete dependence on Murdoch revenue meant that their matches could be (more or less entirely) scheduled to suit subscribers.

Despite having no tradition, no Melbourne-born players, very little crowd support and a completely new team, the Melbourne Storm were initially successful on the field, but the Adelaide side soon disappeared without trace – which, in the mid-term, is likely to be the same fate that befalls the sport. The Murdoch media group has no intrinsic interest in or commitment to rugby league. It's nothing more than a commodity, and – worryingly for rugby league – a commodity whose value is both limited and declining: its audience is almost entirely confined to the east coast of Australia, Auckland and a few other parts of New Zealand, Papua-New Guinea and (rapidly diminishing) pockets of the north of England and the south of France. It has already maximized its television audiences (and subscribers), and there is little or no chance of the game expanding internationally. Australian rules has a much higher media profile, receives more exposure and attracts higher advertising and sponsorship revenue within the Australian market; and the recently launched soccer 'A League' is set to capitalize on the global popularity of that game, the high pop-star status of players with Premier League and Italian Serie A clubs, and Australia's good showing at the 2006 World Cup. The biggest threat to the sport, however, and one that will almost certainly send it into extinction, is the rise of professional rugby union.

Rugby union offers perhaps an even more exemplary case study of the contemporary transformation of a traditional sport into a media-and-business enterprise and spectacle. As we know from previous chapters, union and league split at the end of the nineteenth century over the issue of professionalism, and union culture remained steadfastly amateur and participation-oriented, although shamateurism was rife at international level. In the 1990s, and in response to rugby league consistently poaching its best players, it went professional. The three southern hemisphere powers (South Africa, Australia and New Zealand) came together as SANZAR and signed a lucrative and long-term television rights deals with Murdoch's News Corporation that brought two major competitions into existence – the Tri-Nations (involving home and away internationals) and the Super-10 (then Super-12, now the Super-14, which is made up of provincial sides). This was an example of competitions that completely bypassed the old structures and networks of competition (mostly suburban club games attended by a few thousand spectators, with the occasional interstate or international match): it was set up for television, and financed predominantly through television rights revenue and sponsorship (in 2006 the Super-14 was known by different names in the three countries, corresponding to the company that acquired the naming rights). This development boosted rugby in Australia (at the expense of league) because first it had an international dimension; second, the standard of play increased through the professionalizing of the game and the widespread importation of quality players, particularly from Pacific nations; third, News Corporation heavily publicized the game across the country; and fourth and finally, rugby rules were changed (and refereed in such a way) as to produce entertaining, high scoring games. The consequences for Pacific rugby playing nations, on the other hand, were potentially disastrous: rugby (both fifteen-a-side and Sevens) is a major sport in Fiji, Samoa, the Cook Islands and Tonga, but because none of those had significant media or sponsorship markets they were excluded from both competitions. Further, their best players have tended to move to Australia and New Zealand or to rich northern hemisphere clubs to make a living from the game, and then qualify and play for their adopted home.

In Britain, the close connection between sporting teams and their local populations that had existed in the nineteenth and early twentieth centuries was gradually undermined by radio and television: children growing up in the Midlands of England, Northern Ireland or Wales in the 1920s and 30s, for instance, might well bypass the family tradition of supporting the local team and identify with Herbert Chapman's glamorous Arsenal side. This process accelerated over the last quarter of the twentieth century with the advent of digital communication technology, satellite television and internet sports sites, and the packaging and exporting of competitions (ESPN, for instance, now shows live soccer games from England, Italy, Spain and the Netherlands, as well as NBL, MLB and boxing matches). The increases in the number of regular (televised) international competitions and tournaments, and the levels of coverage and publicity afforded them, gave rise to audiences and fans who never watched their team from the stands, but still wore the colours and/or shirt and followed them on the television screen, or caught real-time scores and coverage on the internet. With the Tour de France, for instance, viewers who have never set foot in France or ridden a bicycle follow each stage and identify with teams and take sides in rivalries.

This 'internationalizing' of interest in and support for teams has its precedents: after the 1958 Munich disaster, Manchester United and the 'Busby Babes' achieved a kind of media status and fan base that transcended local or national boundaries; and the style of play of the Brazilian soccer teams of the 1950s and 60s meant that Brazil came to be more or less associated with the sport. What is different now, however, is the combination of the amount of interest and the income that it generates: Manchester United claim to have approximately fifty million fans worldwide, as well as the support of every fifth soccer fan in the UK; generated US$225 million in revenue in 2002, mainly through television, sponsorship and merchandizing; and has branches all over the UK as well as in Dublin, Belfast, Tokyo and Sydney (Polley 1998: 78). Good results are no longer important for traditional reasons (the need to win trophies, prestige), but because they generate media interest, allow clubs to raise the price of seats, boost season ticket sales, increase the demand for corporate boxes, provide entry into lucrative international competitions, and attract new sponsorship and naming rights money. As well as widening their support base and increasing their revenue globally, there have been major changes in other important areas such as the composition of match day crowds, marketing strategies and their general organizational structure and functions. Spectators, for instance have:

> had to pay more – much more – to be part of the live show. Poorer spectators simply couldn't afford a seat. The 'People's game' was becoming too expensive for the people ... Top clubs changed their shirt designs half a dozen times in as many years ... Clubs believed in charging what the market could bear not what fans could reasonably afford. For all the television money, the price of seats at the big clubs kept rising as fans clamoured to see the new foreign stars ... Entry to big games was increasingly restricted to ticket holders. (Holt and Mason 2000: 106–7)

CASUAL VIEWERS AND CONNOISSEURS

The global interest in professional sport, along with the decrease in the capacity of grounds (a result both of safety legislation and the imperative to provide more comfortable viewing conditions for the middle class/families) and a rise in the cost of attending games, has meant that the experience that supporters and spectators have of professional sport is mediated increasingly through television, newspapers, magazines and new media (the internet, digital phones, etc.) coverage. Moreover, televised sporting contests are watched by an increasing number of casual spectators who "see only violence and confusion" (Bourdieu 1991a: 364). As Bourdieu writes, one only has to think of what is implied:

> in the fact that a sport like rugby (in France – but the same is true of American football in the USA) has become, through television, a mass spectacle, transmitted far beyond the circle of present or past 'practitioners' ... to a public very imperfectly equipped with the specific competence needed to decipher it adequately. The 'connoisseur' has schemes of perception and appreciation which enables him to see what the layman cannot see, to perceive a necessity where the outsider sees only violence and confusion, and so to find in the promptness of a movement, in the unforeseeable inevitability of a successful combination or the near-miraculous orchestration of a team strategy, a pleasure no less intense and learned than the pleasure a music-lover derives from the particularly successful rendering of a favourite work. The more superficial the perception, the less it finds its pleasure in the spectacle contemplated in itself and for itself, and the more it is drawn to the search for the 'sensational'. (1991a: 364)

These new viewers, who are often unfamiliar with rules and traditions and illiterate and/or indifferent with regard to skills, have exercised a considerable influence both over media coverage of sport and the ways it is played. If this viewer is unsure whether, in Bourdieu's terms, the game 'is worth the candle' (2000), it is up to the media and sports administrators to ensure that it is – if only because being (even vaguely or ephemerally) attentive to the sports event provided television ratings and potential audiences for advertising. The first significant attempt to address this imperative came in the 1960s: the American television sports producer Roone Arledge introduced a number of innovations to television sport, including slow motion replays; split screens; halftime analysis and highlights; hand-held close-up shots; situational cameras and microphones; cameras and microphones directed at the crowd to help build a sense of atmosphere; tightly edited packages that increased suspense and eliminated 'slow' play; opinionated 'personalities' as announcers; and Monday Night Football and the 'Wide World of Sports' programme which 'broadened' the definition of sport by including visually spectacular activities such as demolition derbies, cliff diving and Evel Knievel's motorcycle stunts (Roberts and Olson 1997: 418–20). The idea was that "the marriage of sports and innovative entertainment techniques would produce higher ratings" (418). Television had "been content to bring the viewer the game" (418) by using a small number of static cameras. This was enough "for those who loved football, but it was not very attractive to the casual viewer" (418) who had:

> one eye on the screen and one hand on the dial ... Arledge wrote: 'What we set out to do was to get the audience involved emotionally. If they didn't give a damn about the game, they still might enjoy the program'. To do this Arledge used more cameras. He put cameras on cranes and blimps and helicopters to provide a better view of the stadium, the campus, and the town. His technicians developed hand-held cameras for close-ups. In the stadium he employed seven cameras, three just for capturing the environment. 'We asked ourselves: If you were sitting in the stadium, what would you be looking at? The coach on the sideline, the substitute quarterback warming up, the pretty girl in the next section. So our camera wandered as your eyes would'. Often what Arledge decided would interest his mostly male viewers were young and beautiful women ... The game was only one part of the sporting experience. (418)

Although the technical aspects of television coverage have been refined and developed over the last forty years, the approaches and imperatives have remained largely the same. The supposed innovations (bringing in coloured clothing, stump-cameras, white balls, floodlit games, cameras at both ends of the ground and pitch-metres) that characterized Australian television coverage of cricket during the Packer years (in the 1970s) were lauded for making a traditional, complex, nuanced and slow game more dramatic, interesting, relevant and involving for a generalist audience, but the so-called 'Packer revolution' simply brought in variations of techniques or technologies that had been in use in television coverage of American college, NFL and NBA games for almost two decades. Even a recent development such as Skycam – used in the NFL and Australian rules to produce the effect of a soaring and swooping birds-eye view of the action – is just an extension of Ardledge's technology-driven attempt to make sport 'more than itself'.

The use of technologies and techniques that take you 'to the game', along with changes to rules that are designed to make professional sport attractive to a wider demographic, has produced a situation where professional sport now has two quite distinct audiences – Bourdieu's 'connoisseurs' and 'laymen' (1991a: 364). The connoisseur identifies strongly with a team, almost at the level of an idealized abstraction, while the laymen will only identify with and show interest in a sport, team or player when it is fashionable to do so, or when the media hyperbolize an event or story. A good example of both ways of relating – as abstraction and fashionable media entertainment – can be seen in what happened at the 2006 Australian Men's Open. The story of the tournament, as far as media coverage was concerned, was not so much the Cypriot Marco Baghdatis' successful run (beating seeded players such as Andy Roddick and David Nalbandian) as the passionate, colourful and noisy support he received from Melbourne's very considerable Greek community: television coverage, newspaper reports and websites all concentrated on the way Baghdatis played to and fired up the crowd. For the casual viewer tuning in to the final, Baghdatis' opponent Roger Federer was a bit player; his superior skills were at best an irrelevance, and at worst an interruption to a good story. For the serious and literate tennis spectator, however, that skill was the focus of attention, along with comparisons that might be made between Federer and Rod Laver, the last man to win a grand slam (Wimbledon and the Australia, French and US Opens in the same year) – and the player that Federer most resembles technically. While the casual viewer read the tennis match-as-text in terms of Baghdatis' heroics and the crowd antics, the connoisseur reacted to and savoured the moment when Laver presented the trophy to an emotional Federer: their embrace could and would be read as the handing on of tennis' tradition. To the layman, however, the Federer–Laver embrace would only have been significant or worthy of attention if the media coverage, aware that the wheels had fallen off the Baghdatis wagon, had switched their emphasis to (and quickly educated their audience about) Federer's chances of achieving a grand slam.

The same kind of bifurcation can be found in cricket, where commercial and media imperatives have led to the game splitting into three distinct forms: test and first class, one-day and twenty20 matches. Test matches have been played since the mid-nineteenth century: they are scheduled to last five days; there are no limits on how long a team can bat or the number of overs a bowler can bowl; white clothes are worn; and the scoring rate is usually somewhere around two to three runs an over. One-day matches date from the 1970s: they are played in a day or day-night; teams play in coloured clothing; the number of overs (for the batting team and individual bowlers) is limited; and there are additional rules regarding the kind of deliveries that are legitimate, and fielding positions. The twenty20 version is simply a more frenetic version of the one-day game (with innovations such as 'super-subs'), and has only been played on a regular basis over since the new millennium. Test matches usually attract crowds that are highly literate with regard to the rules, skills, techniques and traditions of the game: the long duration (usually from 11am to 6pm each day) and the relatively slow pace of the play where – to the untutored eye – an hour can go by without anything significant happening, makes it unattractive, as well as incomprehensible, to the casual viewer. Test match cricket usually appeals to what we could call a niche market, but the 2005 Ashes series provided a good example of the way in which a traditional sporting form can be brought fully within the media–business nexus. England's improbable victory over

Australia attracted unprecedented television audiences not just in Britain but also in the Indian subcontinent (through the ESPN-Star satellite network), set off a wave of 'Jerusalem' singing not seen since the 1966 soccer World Cup, and gave Andy Flintoff pop star status. This went against the trend, however: test matches have been supplanted in popularity – both in terms of gates and television ratings – by the two limited overs games which take up less time, usually provide a winner (weather permitting), and provide quicker scoring. In terms of an economy of 'time and effect', twenty20 cricket is closer to a soap opera than it is to test cricket: there is a hysterical need to have something dramatic happening constantly.

When something isn't happening in television sport, it's very much up to the commentators to produce something soap-like in its place – passion, drama, scandal, rivalry, heroism, dreams, sex, celebrities, ambition, betrayal, power struggles and intrigue. This imperative frames and narrates media representations of sport: England's preparation for the 2006 World Cup was buried under stories about Sven-Goran Erickson's sexual exploits and/or treachery; and Shane Warne's bowling took a backseat to his mobile phone calls to nurses. This influences how casual viewers see a game: each of Beckham's performances for England, for instance, is analyzed for signs of fashion statements and directions (new hairstyle, etc.), or personal crises (does his lethargy or lack of immediacy on the field presage divorce proceedings?). American sport, because of its long-standing commercial focus, has a tradition of the rogue, self-publicizing sports star providing the game – and the media – with a story, from Muhammad Ali's prophetic poetry to Joe Namath's parties and guarantee of victory, Dennis Rodman's dresses and – most recently – Cincinanni Bengals wide receiver Chad Johnson sending opposition defensive backs tablets to cure the stomach upset and hangover he was promising to give them. In the 2006 NFL Superbowl game between Pittsburgh and Seattle, the lack of any obvious controversy or rivalry threatened to kill off interest in the game except for team fans and NFL devotees: media outlets, desperate for some drama, had to settle for and pick up on little known Pittsburgh linebacker Joey Porter making unconvincing derogatory remarks about the equally low profile Seattle tight end Jeremy Stevens. In the end the biggest story to emerge from the game was, fittingly, Mick Jagger complaining that the sound had been turned down when he was about to sing sexually suggestive lyrics during the Rolling Stones' halftime performance.

INTERACTIVE SPORT

Perhaps the most significant recent development in sports media's attempt to maximize its audience is what is referred to as interactive dimension of contemporary media. BSkyB's digital service, for instance, has a facility that allows viewers to choose their own camera angles and frames, and split the screen to display different games or to show a sporting event and the various betting odds available. As a Premier League game is being played, viewers can edit the coverage while placing bets on incidents in the game (the first player to be sent off, penalty conversion or save) in real time. Another example of sports media interactivity is fantasy sport, which first started in the USA in the 1960s and is played mainly on the internet. Managers draft actual players, or bid for them in auctions, and form virtual squads/teams that usually replicate real numbers and positions (an ice hockey team based on the NHL will have centres, wingers, goalkeepers and defenders). The leagues then take the statistics from NHL games (goals, assists, etc.) and transpose those to fantasy league games. While the Ottawa Senators are beating the Edmonton Oilers by five goals to three, the statistics generated by that game are being used (often immediately) in thousands of fantasy leagues to determine results. Many leagues are hosted by the sports section of large internet news sites (Yahoo, USA Today, Fox, CBS), although an increasing number are run by private providers as businesses; fantasy sport attracts up to thirty million players in America alone (Shipman 2005). They are served by an increasing number of specialist magazines, television sports shows and internet file providers who give advice on who to draft or pick up from the waiver wire, track injuries and statistical variations, and rank players week-to-week according to their fantasy (rather than their actual) value.

Media interactivity in the field of sport functions as both a lure and a way of transforming a viewer's relation to a game. At a basic level it brings audiences into the sports–media mix: so on the BBC Sport website of 29th January 2006 there was a report on the Federer–Baghdatis tennis match which contains, halfway down the page and as part of a 'Have your say' facility, a boxed comment ('From WA') which reads 'Baghdatis should be in the top 20 this year – he gave Federer a hard time in the first two sets'. The comment is inane and the content irrelevant: it's a form of journalese that is too superficial even for the evening television news. The point is that the viewer is now part of the story: 'WA' has made her/his mark within the space of the media analysis and reporting of the match. This attraction is analogous to the lure of talkback radio, where the listener's reactions and opinions are given a public voice and airing, but it also mirrors the phenomenon whereby a sporting crowd attends a game partly in order to watch itself being watched – this is the website equivalent of spotting yourself on the television screen at the ground.

Digital televisions and fantasy sports bring a new level of visual intensity to sports spectatorship – in very different ways. BSkyB's interactive facility is the example par excellence of technology being used to facilitate and incite desire and consumption: in breaking down each minute or aspect of play into a betting opportunity, the spectator is thoroughly and pervasively integrated into what Baudrillard refers to as "a world of generalized hysteria" characterized by a "flight from one signifier to another" (Baudrillard 2003: 77). Within this regime sports, teams, events, players, activities and results are (potentially) rendered as arbitrary and abstracted things with no connection to the field or order of sport, much like the news skit on the 'Two Ronnies' where Ronnie Barker promises to provide the football scores and then simply reads out (relations of) numbers (2-1, 3-0, 2-2, etc.). Or again, it resembles the episode from the 1950s American sitcom 'Sgt Bilko', where the regimental colonel provides the troops with guest speakers who talk about learned topics (history, anthropology) which the entrepreneurial Bilko turns into a gambling game based on how many times the speaker clears his throat.

The BSkyB betting facility hystericizes the act of watching. This is the main difference between gambling on a cricket or boxing match in the eighteenth century and on a soccer game on BSkyB – the latter is seductively interactive. The viewer uses the available technology and her/his presumed literacy to break the game down into signs and sites of consumption (moments, angles, frames, patterns and tendencies) with the promise of returns (both financial and the pleasure of knowing and predicting). This regime of seeing also functions without regard to the gambling facility: the availability of different camera angles and frames across a variety of games draws viewers into the same process whereby they simultaneously consume and become the game: 'WA's' attempt to inscribe her/himself as part of the mediated game on the BBC sports website is carried out, in BSkyB digital, in a much more organized, intensified and consumer-oriented manner.

The lure of interactivity is equally germane to fantasy sport, as are the above observations about spectatorship being both more organized and intense. The keys are control, ownership and identification: a fantasy manager has the status of one god in a pantheon, able to dispose of players (that is, send them to the waiver wire) and acquire them (if they are free agents) at will: but there is also a carry-over from real field of sport, where the adherence to and performance of a general spirit or ethos (fair play), or the pleasure of owning a particular player, is a significant part of the game. So while a fantasy league literally takes sport out of its world or field, and relocates it (players, teams, scores, activities) in an order that is predominantly statistical, the real thing remains a powerful inter-textual influence. When a manager watches an NFL game between Detroit and Chicago, for instance, they may be torn between wanting Detroit (whom they support) to win, while hoping that the Chicago running back on their fantasy team scores a couple of touchdowns; or again, they may draft the Detroit quarterback because they identify with the team, rather than because he is the best player available. Curiously, this intrusion of the discourses, values and ethics of the field of sport (loyalty, fair play and most particularly inalienable identification) is one of the attractions of fantasy leagues: it constitutes a form of play-as-escape from what sport has become (a commercialized, trivialized and hyperbolized media spectacle), albeit one that is usually played out in and through the technologies and spaces of the media-as-business.

CONCLUSION

The Nike commercial that we described and analyzed in our first chapter seems to be suggesting that play and sport are necessarily differentiated: the chaotic activity that erupts before the game starts is quintessential play (it's volitional, wasteful, separated from ordinary life, creative and clearly escapist), but the referee takes charge and forces the players to adhere to the demands of the real, institutionalized game. The message is clear: the strong influence the media, corporate and bureaucratic values, logics and interests (including, of course, Nike's) exert over sport has all but killed off everything that was interesting and valuable about it – whether it was spontaneity, flair, individuality or fun. Simultaneously and contrarily, however, what happens in the tunnel before the game demonstrates that no matter how much the field and its institutions attempt to banish play, it can always return when you least expect it. In other words, the commercial effectively says the opposite of what it purports to say that sport is alive and well, and spontaneous and fun, because the disposition to play never leaves.

Generally speaking, if players started performing, repeatedly and openly, in a non-utilitarian and wasteful manner, they'd probably be substituted, ridiculed by the media and fans, and could even be subject to legal action (they could be accused, for instance, of 'playing dead' and deliberately throwing the game). Certainly the field and its institutions would ensure that what was perceived as consistently wasteful and self-indulgent play would have serious consequences, regardless of the status of the players, because everything is predicated on results. And yet at a discursive level sport specifically and unambiguously elevates, values and commits to principles (such as fair play) that are irreducible to the logics of utility, even after the transformation of sport into media-as-business. There are two closely related examples of this that occurred in English football in the 2000–2001 season. In the first instance, a cup game between Arsenal and Sheffield United, an Arsenal player was injured, and a Sheffield player kicked the ball out to stop the game until he recovered. When the game resumed an Arsenal player threw the ball back to the opposition, but one of his own team members intercepted it and crossed to another teammate, who had 'no choice' but to score – the game was on the line. Arsenal won, but they did so in a manner that contravened the notion of 'fair play'. At the end of the game the Arsenal manager Arsene Wenger apologized and offered Sheffield United a replay, which they accepted. An even more remarkable event occurred a few months later in a game involving West Ham: while the opposition keeper was badly injured, a West Ham player crossed the ball to Paolo di Canio who, instead of heading it into the unguarded net, caught the ball and pointed to the injured player. In both cases the logic of a field dominated by the principles of business (success, self-interest, competitiveness) was rejected in favour of a set of residual principles (clustered around the notion of fair play) that were thought to be more or less extinct.

Footballers acquired, as part of their habitus, a deep-seated attachment to the principle of 'sporting' behaviour. In other words, a 'true sportsperson' will adhere, in words, thoughts, beliefs and actions, to the kinds of values demonstrated by Arsene Wenger (in agreeing to a replay) and Paolo di Canio (in refusing to take advantage of an injured opponent). Now the values exhibited by these two were, as we pointed out earlier, virtually extinct – the fact that what they did elicited such widespread comment and praise demonstrates this. Their behaviour was the exception which proves the rule that the field of sport in fact is dominated by commercial non-principles: managers, players, agents, spectators and journalists typically operate, on a practical level, without regard to a sporting ethos, while maintaining only a discursive commitment to it. In other words it has the status of a kind of Gricean co-operative principle, or set of ideals against which the field and its activities can be measured, judged and critiqued. As Bourdieu explains, while the Gricean principle "is constantly flouted" it functions as "a kind of implicit presupposition of all conversation … which, though it is constantly transgressed, can be evoked at any time, as a reminder of the tacitly accepted rule or an implicit reference to what a conversation has to be in order to be a real dialogue" (2000: 122). The sporting ethos survives precisely because the field is unthinkable without it, and concomitantly because it is the foundation of sport-as-commodity for media and business interests.

The relationship between the disposition to play and those cultural fields and logics closely connected to sport (capitalism, government, the media) constitutes a slightly different and more ambiguous case. Playfulness – as distinct from the ethos of 'fair play' – can be considered valuable and attain the status of a commodity even in professional, utility-driven contexts. It's a relatively rare phenomenon, but there are a number of examples of this (wasteful play inhabiting professional sport) in English and world football in the last forty years. Rodney Marsh of Queens Park Rangers and Matt Le Tissier of Southampton were favourites with the fans, but often berated by managers and sports analysts because of their penchant for 'playing' to a different logic than that of the team. Both were highly skilful – but idiosyncratic and self-indulgent – players who found it difficult to fit into game plans and rarely did the 'workmanlike' tasks their managers expected of them (tackling back or helping out the defence when the team was under pressure, not taking risks in tight situations). They could score spectacular goals, and were capable, on their day, of winning a game on their own; but they are often remembered for their non-utilitarian contributions (juggling the ball in the middle of an intensely competitive game; making an opponent look stupid by beating him more than once). Non-English examples include the Colombian goalkeeper Rene Higuita, who once let a shot sail over his head so he could mule-kick it from behind his back, and the Bulgarian international Dimitar Yakimov who, in the middle of a 1966 World Cup game against Brazil, went off on a mazy dribble that took him past player after player (sometimes twice) to absolutely no effect – save for the obvious pleasure of doing it.

Play abides, but almost always in someone else's place. In *The Practice of Everyday Life* (1988) Michel de Certeau uses binaries such as place/space and strategies/tactics to explicate the relationship between valorized and authoritative institutions and their agents, and those who are, precisely because of power differentials, obliged to perform compliance with regard to those official regimes. So a factory, bureaucracy, church or, say, a professional sport are simultaneously places (maintained and guaranteed by networks of power and capital, and able to dictate or negotiate the rules of practice to those who deal with and inhabit them) and spaces (which is what a place becomes when it is put to unofficial uses, such as a worker using company property for personal ends, or a fan following and identifying with a team which is run as a business). Places make use of strategies, which Certeau describes as "the calculus of force-relationship" which becomes possible when an institution attains relative autonomy within and "can be isolated from an environment" (Certeau 1988: xix). Spaces, on the other hand, are inhabited by tactics or calculations "which cannot count on a spatial or institutional location" (Certeau 1988: xix). The disposition to play necessarily manifests itself within the world and its cultural fields, most of which are distinctly disinclined to take or tolerate it on its own terms. There are some places (the family, child-care centres) where play of-and-for-itself is not just allowed but even encouraged, but these institutions and contexts are mainly associated with children, who are partly exempt from incorporation into the logic of a closed economy.

There are times and places that are set aside for play (weekends and holidays; sports fields and resorts), despite this kind of regimentation being antithetical to the notion of play as spontaneous and volitional. Sporting organizations host play on their own terms, both overtly (witness the rules and regulations concerning, say, what sports spectators may or may not do in different places at different times) and otherwise (hence the organization of 'spontaneous' activity on the part of crowds). In this regulated environment, play is very much like Certeau's tactic that "insinuates itself into the other's place, fragmentarily, without taking it over in its entirety, without being able to keep it at a distance" (Certeau 1988: xix). If play is forced to operate in another place, that is to say within institutions that endeavour to colonize it, then two things become apparent. First, play necessarily takes on forms that would seem, from the perspective offered by Roger Caillois (2001), to constitute its antithesis (work, capitalism, regimentation). Second and concomitantly, the places supposedly operating within the logic of a closed economy are not always what they seem – they are sometimes sites and spaces of waste and dissipation. The American sports sociologist and historian Allen Guttmann points out that:

> Moments of play appear unpredictably in the most unlikely places, even upon the gallows ... In the film Cool Hand Luke, a group of convicts bewilders the guards by increasing the tempo of their road-work, by running back and forth in eager performance of their imposed tasks, by laughing, by turning punishment into play ... Had the convicts begun the game purely for their own amusement ... the activity would have been ... phenomenologically indistinguishable from the utilitarian work that was done. (1978: 13–14)

This imbrication of play with its other leads to the question of whether it is possible to distinguish play at all. Some forms of play remove themselves, materially, temporally and psychologically, from contexts that intrude upon play's volitional nature (Caillois' notion of play-as-ilinx, for instance, is predicated on an attempt to escape from or "destroy reality with sovereign brusqueness") (2001: 23). But rather than distinguish between the generic features of play and certain contexts (work, professionalism, institutionalism), it is more useful to analyze the relationship between play as a disposition and genre, and the different socio-cultural uses to which it is continually being put. In this we are following Arjun Appadurai, who points out that it is impossible to definitively allocate things and practices to one particular economic category (gift or commodity), precisely because they continue to circulate, and are appropriated and reinterpreted, within different socio-cultural contexts (1988).

We can do much the same with play and suggest that something is in a play situation or phase when its socially relevant features are commensurate with the imperatives and generic characteristics outlined by theorists such as

Huizinga and Caillois (it must be separated from ordinary life in some way; non-productive; volitional; adhere to its own rules or logic; and constitute a form of escape from everyday routines), rather than with those of antithetical regimes (such as capitalism, in which case exchangeability would be its socially relevant feature). But while we can accept that play has its own generic features, this is not the same as saying that it has (had) a stable meaning. If the manifestations of and the disposition to play move in and out of the commodity situation, for instance, then one person's escape will become another person's profit, and vice versa. Moreover, in a cultural field such as sport where play has a significant discursive status (play is clearly central to sport's foundation narrative) but is at odds with dominant forms of cultural capital (derived from economics/capitalism), its meanings and functions are likely to be relatively contingent and the subject of (non-playful) agonistics. So, rather than understanding sport as having been animated, at some historical point, by a now atrophied ludic disposition, we can think of it as a set of sites which, despite the influence exerted upon it by governments, media and capitalism, continues (necessarily) to value, provoke, and provide occasions for the disposition to play.

Bibliography

Adelman, M. (1986) *A Sporting Time*. Urbana: University of Illinois Press.

Adelman, M. (1997) 'The Early Years of Baseball, 1845–60'. In S. Pope (ed.) *The New American Sport History*. Urbana: University of Illinois Press.

Althusser, L. (1977) *Lenin and Philosophy and other Essays*. London: New Left Books.

Anderson, B. (1993) *Imagined Communities*. London: Verso.

Appadurai, A. (1988) 'Introduction: commodities and the politics of value'. In A. Appadurai (ed.) *The Social Life of Things*. Cambridge: CUP.

Appadurai, A. (1997) *Modernity at Large*. Minneapolis: Minnesota University Press.

Areangeli, A. (2003) *Recreation in the Renaissance*. New York: Palgrave.

Baker, W. (1982) *Sports in the Western World*. Totowa, NJ: Rowman & Littlefield.

Bale, J. (1982) *Sport and Place*. London: Hurst.

Bale, J. (2001) *Sport, Space and the City*. Caldwell, NJ: Blackburn Press.

Bale, J. and Cronin, M. (eds) (2003) *Sport and Postcolonialism*. Oxford: Berg.

Bale, J. and Christensen, M. (eds) (2004) *Post-Olympism?* Oxford: Berg.

Bataille, G. (1989) *Visions of Excess*. Minneapolis: University of Minnesota Press.

Bataille, G. (1991) *The Accursed Share: Volume I*. New York: Zone Books.

Bataille, G. (1993) *The Accursed Share: Volumes II and III*. New York: Zone Books.

Baudrillard, J. (1983) *Simulations*. New York: Semiotexte.

Baudrillard, J. (2003) *The Consumer Society*. London: Sage.

Benveniste, E. (1971) *Problems in General Linguistics*. Miami: University of Miami Press.

Bhabha, H. (1994) *The Location of Culture*. London: Routledge.

Birch, D. *et al.* (2001) *Asia: Cultural Politics in the Global Age*. Sydney: Allen & Unwin.

Birley, D. (1995) *Land of Sport and Glory: Sport and British Society 1887–1910*. Manchester: Manchester University Press.

Birley, D. (2003) *A Social History of English Cricket*. London: Aurum Press.

Blake, A. (1996) *Body Language: the Meaning of Modern Sport*. London: Lawrence & Wishart.

Borish, L. (1997) 'Catherine Beecher and Thomas W. Higginson on the Need for Physical Fitness'. In S. Riess (ed.) *Major Problems in American Sport History*. Boston: Houghton Mifflin.

Bourdieu, P. (1989) *Distinction*. London: Routledge.

Bourdieu, P. (1990) *The Logic of Practice*. Cambridge: Polity Press.

Bourdieu, P. (1991a) 'Sport and Social Class'. In *Rethinking Popular Culture*. C. Mukerji and M. Schudson (eds). Berkeley: University of California Press.

Bourdieu, P. (1991b) *Outline of a Theory of Practice*. Cambridge: CUP.

Bourdieu, P. (1991c) *Language & Symbolic Power*. Cambridge: Polity Press.

Bourdieu, P. (1992) *An Invitation to Reflexive Sociology*. Chicago: University of Chicago Press.

Bourdieu, P. (1993a) *Sociology in Question*. London: Sage.

Bourdieu, P. (1993b) *The Field of Cultural Production*. Cambridge: Polity Press.

Bourdieu, P. (1995) *The Rules of Art*. Stanford: Stanford University Press.

Bourdieu, P. (1998) *The State Nobility*. Cambridge: Polity Press.

Bourdieu, P. (2000) *Pascalian Meditations*. Cambridge: Polity Press.

Bourdieu, P. (2005) *The Social Structure of the Economy*. Cambridge: Polity Press.

Boyle, R. and Haynes, R. (1998) 'Sack the Board. Sack the Board. Sack the Board. Sack the Board': Accountants and Accountability in Contemporary English Professional Football Culture. In U. Merkel (ed.) *The Production and Consumption of Sport Cultures*. Eastbourne: Leisure Studies Association.

Boyle, R. and Haynes, R. (2000) *Power Play: Sport, the Media, and Popular Culture*. New York: Longman.

Brailsford, D. (1969) *Sport and Society*. London: Routledge and Kegan Paul.

Brailsford, D. (1991) *Sport, Time and Society*. London: Routledge.

Brohm, J-M (1978) *Sport, a Prison of Measured Time*. London: Ink Links.

Caillois, R. (2001) *Men, Play and Games*. Urbana: University of Illinois Press.

Cameron, A. (1976) *Circus Factions*. Oxford: OUP.

Cardus, N. (1934) *Good Days: a Book of Cricket*. London: Cape.

Carter, J. (1988) *Sports and Pastimes of the Middle Ages*. Lanham: University Press of America.

Carter, J. (1992) *Medieval Games*. New York: Greenwood Press.

Cashmore, E. (1990) *Making Sense of Sport*. London: Routledge.

Cashmore, E. (2000) *Sports Culture: An A-Z Guide*. London: Routledge.

Certeau, M. (1988) *The Practice of Everyday Life*. Berkeley: University of California Press.

Childs, D. (1978) 'The German Democratic Republic'. In J. Riordan (ed.) *Sport under Communism*. London: Hurst.

Coakley, J. and Dunning, E. (eds) (2002) *Handbook of Sports Studies*. London: Sage.

Collins, T. (1998) *Rugby's Great Split*. London: Frank Cass.

Crary, J. (1998) *Techniques of the Observer*. Cambridge, MA: MIT Press.

Crary, J. (1999) *Suspensions of Perception*. Cambridge, MA: MIT Press.

Daddario, G. (1998) *Women's Sport and Spectacle*. London: Praeger.

Danaher, G. *et al.* (2000) *Understanding Foucault*. London: Sage.

Debord, G. (1983) *Society of the Spectacle*. Detroit: Black and Red.

Detienne, M. and Vernant, J.P. (1991) *Cunning Intelligence in Greek Society and Culture*. Chicago: University of Chicago Press.

Dobson, S. and Goddard, J. (2001) *The Economics of Football*. Cambridge: CUP.

Donzelot, J. (1979) *The Policing of Families*. New York: Pantheon Books.

Dunning, E. (ed) (1971) *The Sociology of Sport*. London: Frank Cass.

Dunning, E. *et al.* (1988) *The Roots of Football Hooliganism*. London: Routledge & Kegan Paul.

Dunning, E. and Rojek, C. (eds) (1992) *Sport and Leisure in the Civilizing Process*. Basingstoke: Macmillan.

Dyck, N. (ed.) (2000) *Games, Sports and Cultures*. Oxford: Berg.

Dyreson, M. (1995) 'The Emergence of Consumer Culture and the Transformation of Physical Culture: American Sport in the 1920s'. In D. Wiggins (ed.) *Sport in America*. Champaign, IL: Human Kinetics.

Elias, N. (1993a) 'Introduction'. In N. Elias and E. Dunning (eds) *Quest for Excitement*. Oxford: Blackwell.

Elias, N. (1993b) 'An Essay on Sport and Violence'. In N. Elias and E. Dunning (eds) *Quest for Excitement*. Oxford: Blackwell.

Elias, N. (2000) *The Civilizing Process*. Oxford: Blackwell.

Elias, N. and Dunning, E. (1993) *Quest for Excitement*. Oxford: Blackwell.

Fest, J. (1977) *Hitler*. Harmondsworth: Penguin.

Foucault, M. (1973) *The Order of Things*. New York: Vintage Books.

Foucault, M. (1980) *Power/Knowledge*. New York: Pantheon Books.

Foucault, M. (1995) *Discipline and Punish*. New York: Vintage Books.

Foucault, M. (1997) *Ethics: the Essential Works 1*. London: Allen Lane.

Foucault, M. (1998) *Aesthetics, Method, and Epistemology*. New York: New Press.

Foucault, M. (2003) *Society Must Be Defended*. London: Allen Lane.

Frow, J. (1995) *Cultural Studies & Cultural Value*. Oxford: Clarendon Press.

Frow, J. (1997) *Time & Commodity Culture*. Oxford: Clarendon Press.

Gaffney, C. and Bale, J. (2004) 'Sensing the Stadium'. In P. Vertinsky and J. Bale (eds) *Sites of Sport*. London: Routledge.

Gardiner, E. (1930) *Athletics of the Ancient World*. Oxford: Clarendon Press.

Giulianotti, R. (2005) *Sport: a Critical Sociology*. Cambridge: Polity Press.

Golden, M. (1998) *Sport and Society in Ancient Greece*. Cambridge: CUP.

Goodman, C. (1979) *Choosing Sides*. New York: Shocken Books.

Gorn, E. (1997) 'Sports through the Nineteenth Century'. In A. Pope (ed.) *The New American Sport History*. Urbana: University of Illinois Press.

Guha, R. (2003) *A Corner of a Foreign*. Field: the Indian History of a British Sport. London: Picador.

Guttmann, A. (1978) *From Ritual to Record*. New York: Columbia University Press.

Guttmann, A. (1986) *Sports Spectators*. New York: Columbia University Press.

Guttmann, A. (1988) *A Whole New Ball Game*. Chapel Hill: University of North Carolina Press.

Guttmann, A. (1991) *Women's Sport*. New York: Columbia University Press.

Guttmann, A. (1992) *The Olympics, a History of the Modern Games*. Urbana: University of Illinois Press.

Guttmann, A. (1994) *Games and Empire*. New York: Columbia University Press.

Guttmann, A. (1995) 'Puritans at Play? Accusations and Replies'. In D. Wiggins (ed.) *Sport in America*. Champaign, IL: Human Kinetics.

Guttmann, A. (1996) *The Erotic in Sport*. New York. Columbia University Press.

Guttmann, A. and Thompson, L. (2001) *Japanese Sports*. Honolulu: University of Hawai'i Press.

Hargreaves, J. (1987) *Sport, Power and Culture*. Cambridge: Polity Press.

Hargreaves, J. A. (1994) *Sporting Females*. London: Routledge.

Hay, R. (2003) 'The Last Night of the Poms: Australia as a Postcolonial sporting society?'. In J. Bale and M. Cronin (eds) *Sport and Postcolonialism*. Oxford: Berg.

Hill, J. (2002) *Sport, Leisure & Culture in Twentieth Century Britain*. New York: Palgrave.

Hill, J. and Williams, J. (1996) *Sport and Identity in the North of England*. Keele: Keele University Press.

Hoberman, J. (1984) *Sport and Political Ideology*. London: Heinemann.

Hollier, D. (ed) (1988) *The College of Sociology 1937–39*. Minneapolis: University of Minnesota Press.

Holt, J. (1980) *Sport and Society in Modern France*. Hamden, CT: Archon Books.

Holt, R. (1989) *Sport and the British*. Oxford: Clarendon Press.

Holt, R. and Mason, T. (2000) *Sport in Britain: 1945–2000*. Oxford: Blackwell.

Horne, J. *et al.* (1987) *Sport, Leisure, and Social Relations*. New York: Routledge.

Horne, J. *et al.* (1999) *Understanding Sport*. London: Routledge.

Houlihan, B. (1991) *The Government and Politics of Sport*. London: Routledge.

Houlihan, B. (1994) *Sport and International Politics*. Hemel Hempstead: Harvester Wheatsheaf.

Houlihan, B. (ed.) (2003) *Sport & Society*. London: Sage.

Hughson, J. *et al.* (eds) (2005) *The Uses of Sport*. London: Routledge.

Huizinga, J. (1966) *Homo Ludens*. Boston: Beacon Press.

Ingham, A. and Loy, J. (eds) (1993) *Sport in Social Development*. Champaign, IL: Human Kinetics.

Isenberg, M. (1997) 'The Sullivan–Corbett Championship Fight of 1892 and the Modernization of Ring Promotion'. In S. Riess, *Major Problems in American Sport History*. Boston: Houghton Mifflin.

James, C. (1963) *Beyond a Boundary*. London: Hutchinson.

Jarvie, G. and Maguire, J. (1994) *Sport and Leisure in Social Thought*. London: Routledge.

Jay, K. (2004) *More than just a Game*. New York: Columbia University Press.

Johnson, R. (1993) 'Editor's Introduction'. In P. Bourdieu, *The Field of Cultural Production*. Cambridge: Polity Press.

Kirk, D. (1998) *Schooling Bodies*. London: Leicester University Press.

Kirsche, G. (1997) 'Baseball Spectators, 1855–70'. In S. Riess (ed.) *Major Problems in American Sport History*. Boston: Houghton Mifflin.

Kruger, A. (2004) 'What's the Difference between Propaganda for Tourism or for a Political Regime'. In J. Bale and M. Christensen, *Post-Olympism*. Oxford: Berg.

Laidlaw, C. (1999) *Sport and National Identity: Race Relations, Business and Professionalism in Sport, Society and Culture in New Zealand*. Wellington: Stout Research Centre.

Lefort, C. (1986). *The Political Forms of Modern Society*. Cambridge, MA: MIT Press.

Lester, R. (1997) 'The Rise of the Spectator, the Coach, and the Player at the University of Chicago, 1895–1905'. In S. Riess (ed.) *Major Problems in American Sport History*. Boston: Houghton Mifflin.

Loy, J. and Kenyon, G. (eds) (1969) *Sport, Culture, and Society*. London: Macmillan.

Loy, J. *et al.* (1978) *Sport and Social Systems*. Reading, MA: Addison-Wesley.

Maguire, J. (1999) *Global Sport*. Cambridge: Polity Press.

Maguire, J. and Nakayama, M. (eds) (2006) *Japan, Sport and Society*. London: Routledge.

Mandell, R. (1984) *Sport, a Cultural History*. New York: Columbia University Press.

Mangan, J. (1981) *Athleticism in the Victorian and Edwardian Public School*. Cambridge: CUP.

Mangan, J. (ed.) (1992) *The Cultural Bond: Sport, Empire, Society*. London: Frank Cass.

Mangan, J. (ed.) (1996) *Tribal Identities: Nationalism, Europe, Sport*. London: Frank Cass.

Mangan, J. (1999a) 'Prologue'. In J. Mangan (ed.) *Sport in Europe*. London: Frank Cass.

Mangan, J. (ed.) (1999b) *Sport in Europe*. London: Frank Cass.

Mangan, J. (ed.) (2002) *Reformers, Sport, Modernizers*. London: Frank Cass.

Mangan, J. and Small, R. (eds) (1986) *Sport, Culture, Society*. London: E & FN Spon.

Mason, T. (1980) *Association Football and English Society: 1863–1915*. Brighton: Harvester Press.

Mattelart, A. (2000) *Networking the World: 1794–2000*. Minneapolis: University of Minnesota Press.

Mattelart, A. (2003) *The Information Society*. London: Sage.

Mauss, M. (1988) *The Gift*. London: Routledge.

McIntosh, P. (1987) *Sport and Society*. London: West London Press.

McLean, T. (1983) *The English at Play in the Middle Ages*. Windsor Forest NPD: Kensal Press.

McLuhan, M. (1997) *Essential McLuhan*. London: Routledge.

Merkel, U. *et al.* (eds) (1998) *The Production and Consumption of Sport Cultures*. Eastbourne: Leisure Studies Association.

Miller, S. (2004) *Ancient Greek Athletics*. New Haven: Yale University Press.

Money, T. (1997) *Manly and Muscular Diversions*. London: Duckworth.

Morgan, W. (1994) *Leftist Theories of Sport*. Urbana: University of Illinois Press.

Murphy, P. *et al.* (2002) 'Figurational Sociology and its Application to Sport'. In J. Coakley and E. Dunning (eds) *Handbook of Sports Studies*. London: Sage.

Oriard, M. (1993) *Reading Football*. Chapel Hill: University of North Carolina Press.

Patterson, B. (ed.) (1999) *Sport, Society & Culture in New Zealand*. Wellington: Stout Research Centre.

Phillips, D. and Pritchard, D. (eds) (2003) *Sport and Festival in the Ancient Greek World*. Swansea: The Classical Press of Wales.

Plass, P. (1995) *The Game of Death in Ancient Rome*. Madison: University of Wisconsin Press.

Plumb, J. (1974) *The Commercialization of Leisure in Eighteenth Century England*. Reading: University of Reading Press.

Polanyi, K. (1957) *The Great Transformation*. Boston: Beacon Press.

Poliakoff, M. (1987) *Combat Sports in the Ancient World*. New Haven: Yale University Press.

Polley, M. (1998) *Moving the Goalposts*. London: Routledge.

Pope, S. (ed.) (1997) *The New American Sport History*. Urbana: University of Illinois Press.

Redekop, P. (1988) *Sociology of Sport: an Annotated Bibliography*. New York: Garland.

Redhead, S. (1997) *Post-Fandom and the Millennial Blues: The Transformation of Soccer Culture*. London: Routledge.

Ricoeur, P. (1986) *Lectures on Ideology and Utopia*. New York: Columbia University Press.

Riess, S. (1995) *Sport in Industrial America*. Wheeling, IL: Harlan Davidson.

Riess, S. (ed.) (1997a) *Major Problems in American Sport History*. Boston: Houghton Mifflin.

Riess, S. (1997b) 'Sport and the Redefinition of Middle-Class Masculinity in Victorian America.' In S. Pope, *The New American Sport History*. Urbana: University of Illinois Press.

Rigauer, B. (1981) *Sport and Work*. New York: Columbia University Press.

Riordan, J. (ed.) (1977) *Sport in Soviet Society*. Cambridge: CUP.

Riordan, J. (1978a) 'The USSR'. In J. Riordan (ed.) *Sport Under Communism*. London: Hurst.

Riordan, J. (ed.) (1978b) *Sport Under Communism*. London: Hurst.

Riordan, J. and Kruger, A. (eds) (1999) *The International Politics of Sport in the 20th Century*. New York: Routledge.

Roberts, R. and Olson, J. (1997) 'The Roone Revolution'. In D. Wiggins (ed.) *Sport in America*. Champaign, IL: Human Kinetics.

Roche, M. (ed.) (1998) *Sport, Popular Culture and Identity*. Verlag Aachen: Meyer & Meyer.

Rojek, C. (1993) *Ways of Escape*. London: Macmillan.

Sansone, D. (1988) *Greek Athletics and the Genesis of Sport*. Berkeley: University of California.

Schirato, T. and Webb, J. (2004) *Understanding the Visual*. London: Sage.

Shipman, F. (2005) 'Blending the Real and Virtual: Activity and Spectatorship in Fantasy Sports' http://www.csdl.tamu.edu/~shipman/papers/dac01.pdf.

Spivey, N. (2004) *The Ancient Olympics*. Oxford: OUP.

Standish, B. (1997) 'Dick Merriwell Saves the Game'. In S. Riess (ed.) *Major Problems in American Sport History*. Boston: Houghton Mifflin.

Struna, N. (1997) 'Gender and Sporting Practice in Early America, 1750–1810'. In D. Wiggins (ed.) *Sport in America*. Champaign, IL: Human Kinetics.

Sweet, W. (1987) *Sport and Recreation in Ancient Greece*. Oxford: OUP.

Tomlinson, A. (1999) *The Games Up: Essays in the Cultural Analysis of Sport, Leisure and Popular Culture*. Aldershot: Ashgate.

Tranter, N. (1998) *Sport, Economy and Society in Britain. 1750–1914*. Cambridge: CUP.

Vernant, J.P. (1990) *Myth and Society in Ancient Greece*. New York: Zone Books.

Vernant, J.P. and Vidal-Nanquet, P. (1988) *Myth and Tragedy in Ancient Greece*. New York: Zone Books.

Vertinsky, P. and Bale, J. (eds) (2004) *Sites of Sport*. London: Routledge.

Vincent, T. (1994) *The Rise and Fall of American Sport*. Lincoln: University of Nebraska Press.

Volosinov, V.N. (1986) *Marxism and the Philosophy of Language*. Cambridge, MA: Harvard University Press.

Westerbeek, H. and Smith, A. (2003) *Sports Business in the Global Marketplace*. New York: Palgrave.

Whannell, G. (2002) *Media Sport Stars*. London: Routledge.

Wiedmann, T. (1992) *Emperors and Gladiators*. London: Routledge.

Wiggins, D. (ed.) (1997) *Sport in America*. Champaign, IL: Human Kinetics.

Williams, J. (1999) *Cricket and England*. London: Frank Cass.

Williams, J. (2001) *Cricket and Race*. Oxford: Berg.

Index